ESSAYISTS PAST AND, PRESENT

ESSAYISTS PAST AND PRESENT

*A Selection of English Essays, Edited, with
an Introduction and Notes*

BY
J. B. PRIESTLEY

Essay Index Reprint Series

BOOKS FOR LIBRARIES PRESS, INC.
FREEPORT, NEW YORK

First Published 1925
Reprinted 1967

LIBRARY OF CONGRESS CATALOG NUMBER:
67-30227

TABLE OF CONTENTS

5

ESSAYISTS PAST AND PRESENT

INTRODUCTION

THE simplest and safest definition of the essay is that it is the kind of composition produced by an essayist. This does not seem helpful until we reflect that actually we do know what is meant by an essayist, whereas the term " essay " is so elastic that it means nothing. Dr. Johnson defined the essay as " a loose sally of the mind, an irregular, indigested piece, not a regular and orderly performance." But nobody could refer to Locke's great work on the Human Understanding or John Stuart Mill's analysis of Liberty, both of which are called essays by their authors, as loose sallies of the mind or irregular and disorderly performances. Nor could anybody pretend that the essays of Bacon are irregular, indigested pieces. It is impossible to define the essay in terms of either subject or length, for essays exist on all manner of subjects and vary in length from a page or so to several volumes. It is impossible even to confine the essay to prose, for Pope wrote his " Essay on Criticism " and

7

his " Essay on Man " in heroic couplets. The
historian, the philosopher, the politician, the
scientist, the schoolboy, all write essays. But
though all such persons write essays, we do
not call them essayists ; we only call those
writers essayists who produce a certain type
of essay. All the writers gathered together in
this book are essayists, and the things they
write are really and truly essays and it is a
pity that other types of prose composition,
which could easily be given such a title as
"theme," "thesis," or "article," should bear
the name.

De Quincey once made a famous distinction
between what he called the Literature of
Knowledge and the Literature of Power. The
true essay belongs to the latter class. The
mark of our attitude towards the essayist is
that we are indifferent to his subject. It is
he and not his subject that engages us. This
sweeps away, at one blow, all the philosophers
and historians and scientists masquerading as
essayists ; their work, if it belongs to literature
at all, belongs to the Literature of Knowledge.
They write to give us an adequate learned
account of some matter or to prove something,
and if we do not happen to be interested in
the subjects about which they write, we do
not read their work. But the real essayist
has no subject, or, if you will, has every

subject in the world at his command, for the
simple reason that his business is to talk
about himself or to express the relation between any subject and himself. Thus, he can
write, probably delightfully, on a topic about
which he is completely ignorant, because he
will simply discuss his ignorance. The true
essay approximates to familiar talk, and the
essayist is the brilliant and self-revealing
conversationalist, whose every phrase is salted
with personality. Whatever is possible in a
short passage of talk is a possible subject for
an essay. A reminiscence, a fragment of
autobiography, a report of some experience,
an idea and some instances, a character sketch,
and so forth, these are the things that make
up the conversation of a good talker, and
these are the things that make up the subject
matter of the essayist. Because he aims at
the effect of brilliant or familiar and revealing
talk, the success of the essayist depends
largely on manner and style. He is compelled to make the printed word do the work
of the spoken word. The inflections of the
voice, the gestures, the very physical presence
of the talker himself, his face lighting up or
clouding over as he passes from one mood to
another, all these are lost, and cold print has
to take their place. Therefore, in the work of
the major essayists, we should not be surprised

to find a very personal manner and style; the whole writing is saturated with the individuality of its creator, who has contrived to be more himself in print than he is in his own person and talk. Lamb's essays, for example, are not merely the expression of Lamb, they are the essence of Lamb.

If we hold this view of the essay, we shall agree that nothing could be more absurd than the charge of egotism sometimes brought by foolish reviewers against the essayist. If an essayist is not egotistical, he is nothing. The writers who are not egotistical, who do not turn the essay into a receptacle for their whimsical confessions but merely examine a subject at length, are not essayists at all. Even Sir Edmund Gosse, whose article on the Essay in the Encyclopædia Britannica should be read by everybody interested in the subject, makes the mistake of referring to such writers as Jeffrey and Macaulay as essayists. But we shall never get any further and might as well banish the term " essayist " entirely unless we realise that neither of these writers was an essayist. One was a literary critic, the other a literary critic and historian. Their work belongs to the Literature of Knowledge. They wrote to give an account of something, to prove something, to tell us about Crabbe's verse or the War of the Spanish Succession.

INTRODUCTION

In short, they wrote—shall we say ?—
" articles," certainly not essays. As a great
many essayists have been literary critics as
well, there has been a great confusion between
the essay and the critical article. Thus, a
recent anthology of "Modern Essays," in five
volumes, is not really a collection of essays
at all but mainly a collection of critical
articles. If an essayist, such as Hazlitt, is
also, at times, a critic, it naturally follows
that his essays will probably have a critical
flavour just as his critical articles will have
an " essayish " flavour ; as he is a literary
critic, if he expresses his personality in his
essays, the literary critic will out ; nevertheless
a critical article is not an essay if it is to
remain a critical article, and further the
functions of essayist and of literary critic not
only do not go together but actually cancel one
another out, that is to say, a man cannot be
exercising one adequately without definitely
excluding the other. We are always apt to
fall into the error of supposing that because it
is difficult to draw a hard and fast line between
two things, there is little or no difference
between them. But though it is difficult to
tell when the day begins and the night ends
or when the day ends and the night begins, we
do recognise in fact that day and night are
not the same. The functions of essayist and

of literary critic are not, of course, so dia-
metrically opposed, but nevertheless they are
fundamentally different. Not only are many
so-called essayists simply literary critics, but
here and there are certain so-called literary
critics who are really nothing but essayists of
a certain kind. Thus, Anatole France was
really an essayist in his four volumes of so-
called criticism, because to him a book or
an author was merely an excuse to present
himself precisely in the manner in which the
typical essayist presents himself.

Literary historians spend too much time
investigating the origins and early examples
of a literary form; they are so interested in
the roots that they have little time to spare
for the fruits. Thus in their accounts of the
Novel our professors will devote chapter after
chapter to a discussion of Greek and Latin
fables, of medieval romances, of the early
attempts at prose fiction by such writers as
Nash and others, until they have hardly any
space left by the time the novel really begins.
Historians of the Essay have had a tendency
to make the same mistake. The Essay is a
comparatively modern form, like the Novel,
and the last hundred years of its history are
the most important. But the origins are not
without interest. Two names stand out at
the beginning, those of Montaigne and Bacon.

INTRODUCTION

Like the Morris Dance, the Essay is a form of
art that we have brought into this country
from abroad and made our own, for it was
Montaigne, the French gentleman and retired
magistrate, who withdrew to his castle in 1571
for the purpose of writing, with infinite labour,
what we now recognise to be the earliest
essays. Of these " Essais " (for so he called
them, meaning that they were attempts or
trials), the author remarked : " I desire therein
to be delineated in mine owne genuine, simple
and ordinary fashion, without contention, art
or study ; for it is my selfe I pourtray."

The root of the whole matter is there in that
final phrase.

These essays immediately won for themselves an esteem and affection they have never
lost. In 1603, Florio's translation of them
into English appeared, and was undoubtedly
read by Shakespeare, among others. But
Bacon had already published ten of his essays
six years before this. It cannot be said, however, that Bacon carried the essay form any
further ; indeed, the note of intimacy which
marks Montaigne's best work was lost among
the grave and weighty aphorisms of the Lord
Chancellor. The true line of descent is from
Montaigne and not from Bacon, though
English prose composition owes a great deal
to the latter. Detached thoughts on a given

subject, delivered in an impersonal tone, are not to be considered essays, and such were Bacon's "Essays," but they brought the real essay in English a little nearer, with Montaigne always there, as notable an inspiration as his own incomparable wine of Yquem.

During the seventeenth century there were three types of prose writing that were bringing the essay ever nearer. There were first the aphoristic writers who carried on the Bacon tradition, such as Ben Jonson (in his " Timber or Discoveries "), Selden, in his " Table Talk," and others like Sir William Cornwallis. Then there were the character writers, such as Bishop Hall, Sir Thomas Overbury, John Earle, George Herbert, and others, who published between them over fifty collections of little character studies, sketches of types (sometimes dealing with character—" A Discontented Man," " A Contemplative Man," and so forth ; and sometimes merely with rank or profession—" An Alderman," " A Grave Divine," and so on) during the course of the century. These character writers are now only read because they throw a light on the social history of their time and because their work has a certain quaintness, like some queer stiff little engraving on wood, a quaintness, of course, that was not apparent to contemporaries. For the rest, these character

sketches, dealing as they do with broad types
and not with individuals, soon become dull
and monotonous to all but the close student
of the period. But they are of some importance in the history of the essay because the
essayists, when they arrived, did not disdain
the character sketch themselves, though they
turned to individuals rather than broad
types. We have only to compare, say, Earle's
" A Meere Gull Citizen " with Goldsmith's
Beau Tibbs and then with Lamb's delightful
Captain Jackson, to mark the natural evolu-
tion, the movement towards individuality.
In addition to the aphoristic writers and the
character writers, there was a third set of
seventeenth century authors who played an
important part in the history of the essay.
These were the meditative prose-writers, such
as Drummond (in his " Cypress Grove "),
Burton and his " Anatomy of Melancholy,"
and, above all, Sir Thomas Browne, who was
really a born essayist. The richly-imaged and
very musical style of these writers had no
great influence upon the first group of essayists
proper, those of the eighteenth century,
because prose style moved away from them
in the direction of elegance and simplicity ;
but when the romantics came along and
turned their backs upon the eighteenth century, the richer and deeper strain of this

seventeenth century prose caught their ears. Hazlitt's prose is as richly brocaded with imagery as that of Burton or Jeremy Taylor, and amid the lovely jangle of Lamb's bauble and bells we can catch echoes of the strange cadences of Sir Thomas Browne.

But long before the century was spent, the essay can be said to have fairly begun, for by 1688 Abraham Cowley had published " Several Discourses by way of Essays." In one of these, " Of Myself," we get at last that personal interest and appeal which are the very soul of the essay. When Cowley describes how there was wont to lie in his mother's parlour the works of Spenser, and how he came upon the books when he was still a small child and delighted in their fables of knights and giants and monsters, so that " by degrees with the tinkling of the rhyme and the dance of the numbers " he came to read Spenser all through before he was twelve years old— when Cowley is writing like this among the frigid philosophers and the posturing wits, the great essayists may be said to be stirring in the womb of Time. It was only filial piety in Lamb to praise Cowley as enthusiastically as he did. But this directly personal appeal, flashing like a kingfisher through the sedate and exquisitely tended garden of Cowley's prose, is not there in sufficient strength to bring Cowley in to the ranks of the major essayists. His body of work is very slight ; there is too much verse mingled with the prose ; and though a definite personality is there, haltingly expressing itself, there are too many stock subjects treated in the stock manner of the time. The first step has been taken ; the threads have been loosely gathered together ; but that is all. Meanwhile, a number of excellent prose writers, such as Dryden, Halifax, Temple, had discarded the very ornate and (for any ordinary purpose) very cumbersome style of the earlier part of th century and had begun to write a prose that was fitted for everyday work, a simple straightforward style in which a man could tell a story or describe an incident or debate or moralise just as he pleased. This was a notable step forward. When this plain prose had been practised for some time, there came along one of its masters, Defoe, and with him came the periodical.

The history of the essay is inextricably entwined with the history of the periodical. Since there have been papers and magazines to write for, all our chief essayists have been " periodical writers." To anyone with any knowledge of literary history, there is nothing more amusing than the not infrequent complaints of critics and reviewers, who imagine that they are standing for the dignity of letters, against the practice of collecting contributions to the Press, essays or critical articles, and making books of them. We are always led to infer that this is a new and reprehensible practice, a mark of a degenerate age. The truth is, of course, that practically all the best essays in the language have first seen the light in the periodical press. Nearly all the essays in this volume, and certainly the best of them, were written in the first place for newspapers or magazines. From Steele to Mr. Chesterton, from Addison to Mr. Robert Lynd, our essayists have written steadily for the Press. There is not space here to examine this connection between the periodical and the essay, to determine exactly what influence the periodical has had upon the essay, but it is easy to see that the coming of the periodical, which offered a ready market for his contributions, not only smoothed the financial path of the essayist but also offered an inducement to the professional man of letters to turn his attention to this kind of work. The economic influence is easy to understand. What is not so easy to understand is the influence this periodical work has had upon the essayist's attitude of mind, and there is not space here to give it the attention it really deserves. Putting it shortly,

however, we can say that the periodical,
though it frequently restricted the essayist in
both subject matter and his treatment of his
subjects, really gave him a certain confidence
and freedom he would not otherwise have
had.   When a man is writing regularly in one
place for one set of readers (and nearly all the
essayists were regular contributors to the
Press, appearing in the same periodical at
regular intervals), he tends to lose a certain
stiffness, formality, self-consciousness, that
would inevitably make its appearance if he
were writing a whole book at once.   He comes
to feel that he is among friends and can afford,
as it were, to let himself go, and the secret of
writing a good essay is to let oneself go.   It
may be objected that the eighteenth century,
when the periodical essayists, the Ramblers
and Connoisseurs and Adventurers and Idlers,
were in their glory, does not show us many
examples of this lack of stiffness and formality ;
but it must be remembered that stiffness and
formality were the fashion of the moment in
writing and the essayists were at least less
stiff and formal than other men of letters.
Not only did periodical writing encourage the
essayist to feel that he was addressing a
company of friends, so that he lost his self-
consciousness, it also encouraged him to focus
his attention upon little passing things that

he might have disdained were he not writing for the next week's paper. He wrote, so to speak, as he lived; whatever engaged him at the time was likely to find its way into his next essay; and all this tended to bring out the natural man, the real personality of the writer, on which the essay, if it is to be worth anything, must feed. As for the little passing things, some part of the day's show, it may be an odd remark, a quaint figure, a pretty sight, it is not the least part of the good essayist's glory that he takes such homely and seemingly trivial things and in his own lounging, easy fashion links them up to a whole vision of life. He is a snapper-up of unconsidered trifles, and it is his pleasure and privilege to glimpse the significance of such trifles, so that for a second we see them, surprisingly, against the background of the Eternities. He is the poet, his instrument laid aside, musing over a pipe. He is the philosopher on the hearth. And the periodical undoubtedly helped him to sustain this notable part.

When Sir Andrew Aguecheek's attention was called to the "admirable fooling" of his friend, Sir Toby, he remarked: "Ay, he does well enough if he be disposed, and so do I too: he does it with a better grace, but I do it more natural." In the matter of essay writing, Addison, we may say, plays Sir Toby to his

INTRODUCTION

friend Steele's Sir Andrew. Addison did it with a better grace, but Steele did it more natural. The periodical essay begins with these two names, and it is difficult to declare which is the more important. Each has his champions. Addison undoubtedly was the greater man of letters, but Steele's is the greater name in the history of the essay. He was the originator, and though Addison did as much on the *Tatler* and a great deal more on the *Spectator* than Steele did, and had at once more art and more variety in his work, nevertheless it was Steele, happy-go-lucky artless Dick Steele, who carried the essay nearer to perfection, just because he was able at times to escape from the age in which he lived, able to throw away the great wig, the ruffles, the fine satin coat, the cool genteel manner, and to be his simple self, to " do it more natural." In his " Recollections of Childhood " we have the natural man speaking, and speaking with exquisite pathos. But apart from this one essay, the best of both the *Tatler* and *Spectator* papers are easily the little character sketches of Sir Roger de Coverley and his circle. However much the editor of a representative collection of English essays may desire to present fresh material and avoid hackneyed examples of the art, and no matter how carefully he goes through his thick volumes of the *Tatler* and *Spectator* the result is always the same: the Sir Roger papers show like mountain peaks and all else is monotonous lowland. There are exquisite touches here and there, particularly in Steele's papers (it may be a description of a girl selling cherries or of a footman and a maid cleaning the opposite sides of a window and busy making love at the same time), but they are nothing more than isolated paragraphs and not whole essays. Yet if we doubt the genius of these two writers we have only to explore further into eighteenth century periodical writing, after their time, when writers had at least good examples in front of them, to set any such doubt on one side. Steele and Addison raised the periodical essay into such popularity that after them came the deluge. But it was a very dry deluge.

It has been calculated that there were over two hundred papers of the *Tatler* type produced during the eighteenth century. The best known are the *Guardian*, the *Rambler*, the *Adventurer*, the *World*, the *Connoisseur*, the *Idler*, the *Bee*, the *Mirror*, and the *Lounger*. Practically every prose writer of any importance, and not a few poets, wrote papers for these periodicals, and a list of contributors would include men of the most splendid and

INTRODUCTION

varied talent, from Doctor Johnson to Lord Chesterfield, from Swift to Sir Joshua Reynolds. Here, it would seem, is the Golden Age of the essay. Yet the net result of all this scribbling, this industry and talent, so far as the essay is concerned, is woefully small. A few outstanding papers by Swift and Johnson, one small and very delightful volume by Goldsmith—and the rest is silence. Only a few students, endangering their eyesight, have ever thoroughly ransacked this great dustheap of eighteenth century periodical writing. Why, after such a strenuous seed-time, should there be so meagre a harvest ? The answer is easy. These writers denied the essay the quickening breath of personality, and so it died. They were learned and sensible and, frequently, acute ; they observed the world about them and moralised on the spectacle with great good sense ; but they never wrote as individuals, they frowned away the wilful, freakish " I," and wrote as if each one were a kind of composite man of the world. They never saw life from the angle of the individual —vain, humble, ridiculous, tragic—but always merely from the angle of a committee of sensible, well-intentioned persons. We have seen that the essay came into being when Montaigne observed, " It is my selfe I pourtray," quickened into fuller life when

Cowley set down, " Of Myself," and leaped
forward again when Steele forgot the coffee-
houses and wrote his recollections of childhood ; in short, it lived when the natural man
cast aside pretence and wrote out of his heart
and fairly interpreted his mind. It drooped
and all but died (Goldsmith, whose combina-
tion of literary genius and happy folly raised
him above mere fashions, kept it alive), when
no man wrote out of his heart or fairly interpreted his mind, but pretended to feel what
he thought he ought, as a decent member of
society, to feel, and thought what he felt he
ought to think, and buried away fully one half
his heart and mind. " In these humble
essaykins," wrote Thackeray (a born essayist,
whose very novels are a kind of vast panoramic
essay), " I have taken leave to egotise. I cry
out about the shoes which pinch me, and, as
I fancy, more naturally and pathetically than
if my neighbour's corns were trodden under
foot. . . ." The typical eighteenth century
essayist dare not take leave to egotise, and so
wrote gravely on the matter of his neighbour's
corns, and wrote all the more gravely because
his own shoes were pinching him and he dare
not cry out about it.

When we enter the nineteenth century and
the company of the Romantics, the pendulum
has swung back, and now egotism is the fashion

INTRODUCTION

and everybody has pinching shoes and is crying at the top of his voice. The individual has
been rediscovered and is to be found everywhere, explaining and confessing himself.
Revelations are in the air. At the same time,
a richer and more fluid prose has come into
being, challenging poetry on the one side and
the idlest tittle-tattle on the other, an instrument with any number of stops. The essay
is ready for its masters, and its masters, Lamb
and Hazlitt, are here. These two, with some
assistance from Leigh Hunt, made the essay
as easy and familiar as talk, and yet made it
by turns humorous, moving, polemical, richly
descriptive, fitting all their moods like a
magical coat. And now that the essay has
become directly expressive of its writer's
personality, we may remark that it has become
something more, for there is now a tendency
on the part of the essayist, as it were, to
dramatise himself in his work, deliberately to
heighten and colour his mind and temperament in the manner adopted by novelists who
turn real people of their acquaintance into
characters for their novels. Hazlitt loved
and hated strongly enough in his real life,
but he never loved and hated with the fervour
of the Hazlitt of the essays. Lamb was
capricious and whimsical enough among his
friends, but he was not so capricious and

25

whimsical as the Lamb of the essays. The same can be said of every good essayist who has written since. But this process of dramatising oneself is something very different from the cold pretence common in the earlier century; it is simply a heightening and colouring, for purposes of artistic emphasis, of what is already there; it is Lamb, as I have said, simply being more Lamb-ish, not Lamb trying to think, feel and write, let us say, like Godwin; and we who read Hazlitt's essays probably know more about the essential Hazlitt than his acquaintances did. This process has gone on, and it is still going on, while there are good essayists left with us. Indeed, after Lamb and Hazlitt, a history of the essay is hardly anything more than a succession of names. There have been new developments, but only comparatively small ones, for these two great writers made the essay into an instrument of power that any man, if he had sufficient art and individuality, could take up and play and so renew its old enchantments. The remaining history of the essay is hardly anything more than a succession of new personalities, new temperaments and new styles. As time wears on, the names grow thicker, but the winnowing is more severe, and only the masters of the strange craft remain.

INTRODUCTION

One tendency common among essayists of our time needs some comment. Many of our contemporary essayists, men of great talent, are both by nature and choice controversialists who have devoted most of their energy to furthering some particular set of ideas and opinions. Now the essay does not by its nature entirely exclude controversy and debate, but it does not encourage them. The debating mood is not the mood in which great essays are written. The born controversialist, after a time, is apt to relate everything in his experience to his opinions, which come to mean, to him, his mind. Genuine autobiography becomes impossible to him. It is not that he is pretending to you, but that he is pretending to himself or has pretended so long that pretence is no longer necessary. When an author of this kind writes essays, he will probably adopt the manner of the essayist proper, but what he is aiming at is something very different. He is not really intent upon portraying himself, giving us the genuine shape and colour of his mind ; his object is to air his opinions, to prove a point, and everything will be compelled to serve that end. We, the readers, journey pleasantly forward in one of his essays until suddenly the cry rings out, " Your acquiescence or your life," and we find ourselves held up by the old gang of opinions, which have been devising the ambush ever since we began. Mr. G. K. Chesterton is perhaps the best example of such writers. He has written extremely brilliant essays and has, indeed, almost every quality necessary to an essayist of the highest rank, but he has long since been seduced by controversy and debate, and the greater number of his essays, full as they are of good things, are ruined by their obvious desire to score debating points. There is in them a lack of genuine autobiography ; we discover at the end of our reading that though our author has hammered his opinions home, he has not made himself plain to us ; the real man is still hidden away. This is not a weakness of which Mr. Chesterton himself is ignorant ; it is plainly the result of deliberate choice. Lively controversy may be more important than " egotising " ; and Mr. Chesterton obviously thinks it is, but an historian or lover of the essay, in spite of some capital examples of the form that Mr. Chesterton has given us (of which there is one in this volume), must shake his head over so notable a deserter from its ranks.

Our own time has been comparatively rich in essayists, though it is yet too early to see them clearly against the background of the English Essay. In addition to the four living

essayists represented in this volume, there is
a numerous company in which Messrs. Beer-
bohm, Birrell, Hewlett, Edward Thomas,
G. S. Street, H. M. Tomlinson, to name no
others, must be given prominent places. There
are, however, disquietening signs that the
periodical, particularly the daily Press (in
which many essayists regularly appeared before
the war), is loosening its old alliance with the
essay. Between the " publicist," with his
streams of debate, on the one hand, and the
journalistic hack, with his snappy little articles
that have no more to do with literature than
has a Gatling gun, on the other, the essay,
with its more leisurely appeal and its greater
demand upon the reader's intelligence, is being
squeezed out of its old columns. This is
probably due in part to the enormous quantity
of bad essays that have made their appearance
from time to time. While there are few
things in literature better than a good essay—
the genuine expression of an original personality—there are few things worse than a
bad one. The faults of the bad essay are
generally connected with an obvious desire
on the part of a writer to imitate, superficially,
some admired essayist. A kind of essay
manner, which makes great use of archaisms
and certain hackneyed tricks of speech, is
cultivated in the hope that it will somehow

transform the writer into a Hazlitt or a Lamb. But Brown will only succeed when he is as much Brown as Hazlitt was Hazlitt or Lamb was Lamb. If the theory of the essay touched on here is held to be the right one, it is obvious that it is fatal to be merely imitative and derivative in the essay, for there everything hangs upon personality and the writer can only succeed by being himself.

The present selection is designed to serve either as an introduction to the more important essayists (and many persons of merit have been reluctantly omitted), or as a pleasant kind of visit to a company of old friends. In making the choice of essays I have had several objects in view. I wanted the essays to make up between them a companionable varied kind of book, and to be representative of the general history of the English Essay and of their several authors. I have deliberately avoided essays that have become hackneyed by too frequent selection. Thus, I have omitted Hazlitt's " On Going a Journey " and its somewhat overpraised and very hackneyed companion, Stevenson's " Walking Tours," which is not so good as the present choice, " The Lantern Bearers," or several others rarely selected. As I have nowhere discussed the actual form of the essay, perhaps I may be allowed to say in this

place that " The Lantern Bearers," along
with one or two of the other essays here, is a
good example of the type of essay, in matter
and form, I prefer. This type of essay begins
with an experience ; it may be some remembrance of childhood or something that
happened yesterday, and then gradually,
almost insensibly, draws out of this experience
some general idea that is then expanded,
touched gently, as it were, with the philosophic
finger and then laid down. Some of my
favourite essays do not proceed in this way,
but this seems to me the most engaging and
fruitful type of essay. For the rest, the three
Lamb essays have been chosen with one eye
on the hackneyed and the other on the many
sides of Lamb that should, if possible, be
represented. The Sir Roger and Beau Tibbs
papers were inevitable, and I make no apology
for including them. It is more than likely
that the essays by Swift and Johnson selected
here will be unfamiliar to most readers, and
perhaps their presence will make up for that
of any too frequent visitors. It should be
hardly necessary to point out, even to those
readers who have spent little time with the
essayists, that a selection of this kind, in
which each essayist has only a few pages to
himself, cannot illustrate with any success the
theory that the essay is the expression of a

personality, an artful and enduring kind of
talk. It cannot do this just because the
essayist has not space enough in which to
make himself felt. The reader, when he has
tasted here, must make his choice and pass on
to the complete volumes. If he is wise he
will entertain all these gentlemen, for he will
find that one or other of them will engage and
distract him whatever his mood may be.
They are among the wisest of authors, and
certainly they are the friendliest, and the
reader who entertains them on his shelves
will discover to his delight that he has for
ever at his elbow, at his command, a most
notable company of talkers who can ease his
pains and mirror his happiness, and whose
very pages will soon begin to look like the
faces of old friends.

J. B. PRIESTLEY.

My thanks are due to Mr. E. V. Lucas, Mr. Hilaire
Belloc, Mr. G. K. Chesterton, Mr. Robert Lynd, and
their publishers, Messrs. Methuen, and to Messrs. Chatto &
Windus and Messrs. Scribners, the publishers of
Stevenson's "Lantern-Bearers," for permission to re-
print the last five essays in this volume.

J. B. P.

ESSAYISTS PAST AND PRESENT

RICHARD STEELE

[1672–1729]

ON DOMESTIC FELICITY

" *Interea dulces pendent circum oscula nati,*
Casta pudicitiam servat domus . . . ."
VIRG., Georg. ii, 523.

" *His cares are eas'd with intervals of bliss ;*
His little children, climbing for a kiss,
Welcome their father's late return at night ;
His faithful bed is crowned with chaste delight."
DRYDEN.

From my own Apartment, November 16

THERE are several persons who have many pleasures and entertainments in their possession, which they do not enjoy. It is, therefore, a kind and good office to acquaint them with their own happiness, and turn their attention to such instances of their good fortune as they are apt to overlook. Persons in the married state often want

C
33

such a monitor ; and pine away their days, by
looking upon the same condition in anguish
and murmur, which carries with it in the
opinion of others a complication of all the
pleasures of life, and a retreat from its
inquietudes.

I am led into this thought by a visit I made
an old friend, who was formerly my school-
fellow. He came to town last week with his
family for the winter, and yesterday morning
sent me word his wife expected me to dinner.
I am, as it were, at home at that house, and
every member of it knows me for their well-
wisher. I cannot indeed express the pleasure
it is, to be met by the children with so much
joy as I am when I go thither. The boys and
girls strive who shall come first, when they
think it is I that am knocking at the door ;
and that child which loses the race to me runs
back again to tell the father it is Mr. Bickerstaff. This day I was led in by a pretty girl,
that we all thought must have forgot me ; for
the family has been out of town these two
years. Her knowing me again was a mighty
subject with us, and took up our discourse at
the first entrance. After which, they began
to rally me upon a thousand little stories they
heard in the country, about my marriage to
one of my neighbour's daughters. Upon
which the gentleman, my friend, said, " Nay,

if Mr. Bickerstaff marries a child of any of his old companions, I hope mine shall have the preference; there is Mrs. Mary is *now sixteen,* and would make him as fine a widow as the best of them. But I know him too well; he is so enamoured with the very memory of those who flourished in his youth, that he will not so much as look upon the modern beauties. I remember, old gentleman, how often you went home in a day to refresh your countenance and dress when Teraminta reigned in your heart. As we came up in the coach, I repeated to my wife some of your verses on her." With such reflections on little passages which happened long ago, we passed our time, during a cheerful and elegant meal. After dinner, his lady left the room, as did also the children. As soon as we were alone, he took me by the hand; "Well, my good friend," says he, "I am heartily glad to see thee; I was afraid you would never have seen all the company that dined with you to-day again. Do not you think the good woman of the house a little altered, since you followed her from the play-house, to find out who she was, for me?" I perceived a tear fall down his cheek as he spoke, which moved me not a little. But, to turn the discourse, I said, "She is not indeed quite that creature she was, when she returned me the letter I carried from

you; and told me, ' she hoped, as I was a
gentleman, I would be employed no more to
trouble her, who had never offended me; but
would be so much the gentleman's friend, as
to dissuade him from a pursuit, which he
could never succeed in.' You may remember,
I thought her in earnest; and you were forced
to employ your cousin Will, who made his
sister get acquainted with her, for you. You
cannot expect her to be for ever fifteen."
" Fifteen ! " replied my good friend : " Ah !
you little understand, you that have lived a
bachelor, how great, how exquisite a pleasure
there is, in being really beloved ! It is impossible, that the most beauteous face in
nature should raise in me such pleasing ideas,
as when I look upon that excellent woman.
That fading in her countenance is chiefly
caused by her watching with me, in my fever.
This was followed by a fit of sickness, which
had like to have carried her off last winter.
I tell you sincerely, I have so many obligations
to her, that I cannot, with any sort of modera-
tion, think of her present state of health.
But as to what you say of fifteen, she gives me
every day pleasures beyond what I ever knew
in the possession of her beauty, when I was
in the vigour of youth. Every moment of
her life brings me fresh instances of her complacency to my inclinations, and her prudence

in regard *to* my fortune. Her face is to me much more beautiful than when I first saw it ; there is no decay in any feature, which I cannot trace, from the very instant it was occasioned by some anxious concern for my welfare and interests. Thus, at the same time, methinks, the love I conceived towards her for what she was, is heightened by my gratitude for what she is. The love of a wife is as much above the idle passion commonly called by that name, as the loud laughter of buffoons is inferior to the elegant mirth of gentlemen. Oh ! she is an inestimable jewel. In her examination of her household affairs, she shows a certain fearfulness to find a fault, which makes her servants obey her like children ; and the meanest we have has an ingenuous shame for an offence, not always to be seen in children in other families. I speak freely to you, my old friend ; ever since her sickness, things that gave me the quickest joy before, turn now to a certain anxiety. As the children play in the next room, I know the poor things by their steps, and am considering what they must do, should they lose their mother in their tender years. The pleasure I used to take in telling my boy stories of battles, and asking my girl questions about the disposal of her baby, and the gossiping of it, is turned into inward reflection and melancholy."

He would have gone on in this tender way, when the good lady entered, and with an inexpressible sweetness in her countenance told us, " she had been searching her closet for something very good, to treat such an old friend as I was." Her husband's eyes sparkled with pleasure at the cheerfulness of her countenance ; and I saw all his fears vanish in an instant. The lady observing something in our looks which showed we had been more serious than ordinary, and seeing her husband receive her with great concern under a forced cheerfulness, immediately guessed at what we had been talking of ; and applying herself to me, said, with a smile, " Mr. Bickerstaff, do not believe a word of what he tells you ; I shall still live to have you for my second, as I have often promised you, unless he takes more care of himself than he has done since his coming to town. You must know, he tells me that he finds London is a much more healthy place than the country ; for he sees several of his old acquaintance and school-fellows are here *young fellows with fair full-bottomed* periwigs. I could scarce keep him this morning from going out *open-breasted.*" My friend, who is always extremely delighted with her agreeable humour, made her sit down with us. She did it with that easiness which is peculiar to women of sense ; and to keep up the good humour she had brought in with her, turned her raillery upon me. "Mr. Bickerstaff, you remember you followed me one night from the play-house; suppose you should carry me thither to-morrow night, and lead me into the front box." This put us into a long field of discourse about the beauties, who were mothers to the present, and shined in the boxes twenty years ago. I told her, I was glad she had transferred so many of her charms, and I did not question but her eldest daughter was within half a year of being a toast.

We were pleasing ourselves with this fantastical preferment of the young lady, when on a sudden we were alarmed with the noise of a drum, and immediately entered my little godson to give me a point of war. His mother, between laughing and chiding, would have put him out of the room; but I would not part with him so. I found, upon conversation with him, though he was a little noisy in his mirth, that the child had excellent parts, and was a great master of all the learning on the other side eight years old. I perceived him a very great historian in Æsop's Fables : but he frankly declared to me his mind, "that he did not delight in that learning, because he did not believe they were true"; for which reason I found he had very much turned his

RICHARD STEELE

studies, for about a twelvemonth past, into
the lives and adventures of Don Bellianis of
Greece, Guy of Warwick, the Seven Champions,
and other historians of that age. I could not
but observe the satisfaction the father took
in the forwardness of his son ; and that these
diversions might turn to some profit, I found
the boy had made remarks, which might be
of service to him during the course of his
whole life. He would tell you the mis-
managements of John Hickerthrift, find fault
with the passionate temper in Bevis of South-
ampton, and loved Saint George for being
the champion of England ; and by this means
had his thoughts insensibly moulded into the
notions of discretion, virtue, and honour.
I was extolling his accomplishments, when the
mother told me, " that the little girl who led
me in this morning was in her way a better
scholar than he. Betty," she said, " deals
chiefly in fairies and sprights ; and sometimes
in a winter-night will terrify the maids with
her accounts, until they are afraid to go up
to bed."

I sat with them until it was very late,
sometimes in merry, sometimes in serious discourse, with this particular pleasure, which
gives the only true relish to all conversation, a
sense that every one of us liked each other. I
went home, considering the different conditions

40

ON DOMESTIC FELICITY

of a married life and that of a bachelor; and I must confess it struck me with a secret concern, to reflect, that whenever I go off I shall leave no traces behind me. In this pensive mood I return to my family; that is to say, to my maid, my dog, and my cat, who only can be the better or worse for what happens to me.

RICHARD STEELE

[1672–1729]

RECOLLECTIONS OF CHILDHOOD

" . . . *Dies, ni fallor, adest, quem semper acerbym,*
Semper honoratum, sic dii voluistis habebo."

VIRG., Æn. v, 49.

" *And now the rising day renews the year,*
A day for ever sad, for ever dear."

DRYDEN.

From my own Apartment, June 5

THERE are those among mankind, who can enjoy no relish of their being, except the world is made acquainted with all that relates to them, and think everything lost that passes unobserved ; but others find a solid delight in stealing by the crowd, and modelling their life after such a manner, as is as much above the approbation as the practice of the vulgar. Life being too short to give instances great enough of true friendship or good-will, some sages have thought it pious to preserve a certain reverence for the names of their deceased friends ; and

42

have withdrawn themselves from the rest of
the world at certain seasons, to commemorate
in their own thoughts such of their acquaintance who have gone before them out of this
life. And indeed, when we are advanced in
years, there is not a more pleasing entertainment, than to recollect in a gloomy
moment the many we have parted with,
that have been dear and agreeable to us, and
to cast a melancholy thought or two after
those, with whom, perhaps, we have indulged
ourselves in whole nights of mirth and jollity.
With such inclinations in my heart I went
to my closet yesterday in the evening, and
resolved to be sorrowful ; upon which occasion
I could not but look with disdain upon myself,
that though all the reasons which I had to
lament the loss of many of my friends are now
as forcible as at the moment of their departure,
yet did not my heart swell with the same
sorrow which I felt at that time ; but I could,
without tears, reflect upon many pleasing
adventures I have had with some, who have
long been blended with common earth.
Though it is by the benefit of nature, that
length of time thus blots out the violence
of afflictions ; yet, with tempers too much
given to pleasure, it is almost necessary to
revive the old places of grief in our memory ;
and ponder step by step on past life, to lead

the mind into that sobriety of thought which poises the heart, and makes it beat with due time, without being quickened with desire, or retarded with despair, from its proper and equal motion. When we wind up a clock that is out of order, to make it go well for the future, we do not immediately set the hand to the present instant, but we make it strike the round of all its hours, before it can recover the regularity of its time. Such, thought I, shall be my method this evening; and since it is that day of the year which I dedicate to the memory of such in another life as I much delighted in when living, an hour or two shall be sacred to sorrow and their memory, while I run over all the melancholy circumstances of this kind which have occurred to me in my whole life.

The first sense of sorrow I ever knew was upon the death of my father at which time I was not quite five years of age; but was rather amazed at what all the house meant, than possessed with a real understanding why nobody was willing to play with me. I remember I went into the room where his body lay, and my mother sat weeping alone by it. I had my battledore in my hand, and fell a beating the coffin, and calling Papa; for, I know not how, I had some slight idea that he was locked up there. My mother catched me in her arms, and, transported beyond all patience of the silent grief she was before in, she almost smothered me in her embraces; and told me in a flood of tears, "Papa could not hear me, and would play with me no more, for they were going to put him under ground, whence he could never come to us again." She was a very beautiful woman, of a noble spirit, and there was a dignity in her grief amidst all the wildness of her transport; which, methought, struck me with an instinct of sorrow, that, before I was sensible of what it was to grieve, seized my very soul, and has made pity the weakness of my heart ever since. The mind in infancy is, methinks, like the body in embryo; and receives impressions so forcible, that they are as hard to be removed by reason, as any mark with which a child is born is to be taken away by any future application. Hence it is, that good-nature in me is no merit; but having been so frequently overwhelmed with her tears before I knew the cause of any affliction, or could draw defences from my own judgment, I imbibed commiseration, remorse, and an unmanly gentleness of mind, which has since insnared me into ten thousand calamities; from whence I can reap no advantage, except it be, that, in such a humour as I am now in, I can the better indulge myself in the softnesses of humanity, and enjoy that sweet anxiety which arises from the memory of past afflictions.

We, that are very old, are better able to remember things which befell us in our distant youth, than the passages of later days. For this reason it is, that the companions of my strong and vigorous years present themselves more immediately to me in this office of sorrow. Untimely and unhappy deaths are what we are most apt to lament; so little are we able to make it indifferent when a thing happens, though we know it must happen. Thus we groan under life, and bewail those who are relieved from it. Every object that returns to our imagination raises different passions, according to the circumstance of their departure. Who can have lived in an army, and in a serious hour reflect upon the many gay and agreeable men that might long have flourished in the arts of peace, and not join with the imprecations of the fatherless and widow on the tyrant to whose ambition they fell sacrifices ? But gallant men, who are cut off by the sword, move rather our veneration than our pity; and we gather relief enough from their own contempt of death, to make that no evil, which was approached with so much cheerfulness, and attended with so much honour. But when we turn our thoughts from the great parts of life on such occasions, and instead of lamenting those who stood ready to give death to those from whom they had the fortune to receive it ; I say, when we let our thoughts wander from such noble objects, and consider the havock which is made among the tender and the innocent, pity enters with an unmixed softness, and possesses all our souls at once.

Here (were there words to express such sentiments with proper tenderness) I should record the beauty, innocence, and untimely death, of the first object my eyes ever beheld with love. The beauteous virgin ! How ignorant did she charm, how carelessly excel ? Oh Death ! thou hast right to the bold, to the ambitious, to the high, and to the haughty ; but why this cruelty to the humble, to the meek, to the undiscerning, to the thoughtless ? Nor age, nor business, nor distress, can erase the dear image from my imagination. In the same week, I saw her dressed for a ball, and in a shroud. How ill did the habit of death become the pretty trifler ? I still behold the smiling earth—A large train of disasters were coming on to my memory, when my servant knocked at my closet-door, and interrupted me with a letter, attended with a hamper of wine, of the same sort with that which is to be put to sale on

Thursday next, at Garraway's coffee-house. Upon the receipt of it, I sent for three of my friends. We are so intimate, that we can be company in whatever state of mind we meet, and can entertain each other without expecting always to rejoice. The wine we found to be generous and warming, but with such a heat as moved us rather to be cheerful than frolicksome. It revived the spirits, without firing the blood. We commended it until two of the clock this morning ; and having to-day met a little before dinner, we found, that though we drank two bottles a man, we had much more reason to recollect than forget what had passed the night before.

RICHARD STEELE
[1672–1729]

OF THE CLUB

" *Ast alii sex,*
Et plures, uno conclament ore."
JUV., Sat. vii, 167.
" *Six more at least join their consenting voice.*"

THE first of our society is a gentleman of Worcestershire, of an ancient descent, a baronet, his name Sir Roger de Coverley. His great grandfather was inventor of that famous country-dance which is called after him. All who know that shire are very well acquainted with the parts and merits of Sir Roger. He is a gentleman that is very singular in his behaviour, but his singularities proceed from his good sense, and are contradictions to the manners of the world, only as he thinks the world is in the wrong. However, this humour creates him no enemies, for he does nothing with sourness or obstinacy ; and his being unconfined to modes and forms, makes him but the readier and more capable to please and

D   49

oblige all who know him. When he is in town, he lives in Soho-square. It is said, he keeps himself a bachelor by reason he was crossed in love by a perverse, beautiful widow of the next county to him. Before this disappointment, Sir Roger was what you call a fine gentleman,. had often supped with my Lord Rochester and Sir George Etherege, fought a duel upon his first coming to town, and kicked bully Dawson in a public coffee-house for calling him youngster. But being ill-used by the above-mentioned widow, he was very serious for a year and a half; and though, his temper being naturally jovial, he at last got over it, he grew careless of himself, and never dressed afterwards. He continues to wear a coat and doublet of the same cut that were in fashion at the time of his repulse, which, in his merry humours, he tells us, has been in and out twelve times since he first wore it. It is said Sir Roger grew humble in his desires after he had forgot his cruel beauty, insomuch that it is reported he has frequently offended in point of chastity with beggars and gypsies : but this is looked upon, by his friends, rather as matter of raillery than truth. He is now in his fifty-sixth year, cheerful, gay, and hearty ; keeps a good house both in town and country ; a great lover of mankind ; but there is such a mirthful cast in his behaviour, that he is rather beloved than esteemed. His tenants grow rich, his servants look satisfied, all the young women profess love to him, and the young men are glad of his company. When he comes into a house, he calls the servants by their names, and talks all the way up stairs to a visit. I must not omit, that Sir Roger is a justice of the quorum; that he fills the chair at a quarter-session with great abilities, and three months ago gained universal applause, by explaining a passage in the game-act.

The gentleman next in esteem and authority among us is another bachelor, who is a member of the Inner Temple, a man of great probity, wit, and understanding; but he has chosen his place of residence rather to obey the direction of an old humorsome father, than in pursuit of his own inclinations. He was placed there to study the laws of the land, and is the most learned of any of the house in those of the stage. Aristotle and Longinus are much better understood by him than Littleton or Coke. The father sends up every post questions relating to marriage-articles, leases and tenures, in the neighbourhood; all which questions he agrees with an attorney to answer and take care of in the lump. He is studying the passions themselves when he should be enquiring into the debates among men which arise from them. He

RICHARD STEELE

knows the argument of each of the orations
of Demosthenes and Tully, but not one case
in the reports of our own courts. No one
ever took him for a fool ; but none, except his
intimate friends, know he has great deal of
wit. This turn makes him at once both
disinterested and agreeable. As few of his
thoughts are drawn from business, they are
most of them fit for conversation. His taste
for books is a little too just for the age he
lives in ; he has read all, but approves of very
few. His familiarity with the customs, manners,
actions, and writings of the ancients, makes him
a very delicate observer of what occurs to him
in the present world. He is an excellent critic,
and the time of the play is his hour of business ;
exactly at five he passes through New-Inn, crosses
through Russel-court, and takes a turn at Will's
till the play begins ; he has his shoes rubbed
and his periwig powdered at the barber's as
you go into the Rose. It is for the good of the
audience when he is at a play, for the actors
have an ambition to please him.

The person of next consideration is Sir
Andrew Freeport, a merchant of great eminence
in the city of London ; a person of indefati-
gable industry, strong reason, and great
experience. His notions of trade are noble
and generous, and (as every rich man has
usually some sly way of jesting, which would

make no great figure were he not a rich man)
he calls the sea the British Common. He is
acquainted with commerce in all its parts,
and will tell you that it is a stupid and barbarous way to extend dominion by arms ;
for true power is to be got by arts and industry.
He will often argue, that if this part of our
trade were well cultivated, we should gain
from one nation ; and if another, from another.
I have heard him prove, that diligence makes
more lasting acquisitions than valour, and
that sloth has ruined more nations than the
sword. He abounds in several frugal maxims,
amongst which the greatest favourite is,
" A penny saved is a penny got." A general
trader of good sense is pleasanter company
than a general scholar ; and Sir Andrew having
a natural unaffected eloquence, the perspicuity
of his discourse gives the same pleasure that we
would in another man. He has made his fortune himself ; and says that England may be
richer than other kingdoms, by as plain methods
as he himself is richer than other men ; though
at the same time I can say this of him, that
there is not a point in the compass, but blows
home a ship in which he is an owner.

Next to Sir Andrew in the club-room sits
Captain Sentry, a gentleman of great courage,
good understanding, but invincible modesty.
He is one of those that deserve very well,

but are very awkward at putting their talents within the observation of such as should take notice of them. He was some years a captain, and behaved himself with great gallantry in several engagements and at several sieges ; but having a small estate of his own, and being next heir to Sir Roger, he has quitted a way of life in which no man can rise suitably to his merit, who is not something of a courtier as well as a soldier. I have heard him often lament, that in a profession where merit is placed in so conspicuous a view, impudence should get the better of modesty. When he has talked to this purpose, I never heard him make a sour expression, but frankly confess that he left the world, because he was not fit for it. A strict honesty, and an even regular behaviour, are in themselves obstacles to him that must press through crowds, who endeavour at the same end with himself, the favour of a commander. He will however in his way of talk excuse generals, for not disposing according to men's desert, or enquiring into it ; For, says he, that great man who has a mind to help me, has as many to break through to come at me, as I have to come at him : therefore, he will conclude, that the man who would make a figure, especially in a military way, must get over all false modesty, and assist his patron against the importunity of other pretenders, by a proper assurance in his own vindication. He says it is a civil cowardice to be backward in asserting what you ought to expect, as it is a military fear to be slow in attacking when it is your duty. With this candour does the gentleman speak of himself and others. The same frankness runs through all his conversation. The military part of his life has furnished him with many adventures, in the relation of which he is very agreeable to the company; for he is never overbearing, though accustomed to command men in the utmost degree below him; nor ever too obsequious, from an habit of obeying men highly above him.

But that our society may not appear a set of humorists, unacquainted with the gallantries and pleasures of the age, we have amongst us the gallant Will Honeycomb; a gentleman who, according to his years, should be in the decline of his life; but having ever been very careful of his person, and always had a very easy fortune, time has made but a very little impression, either by wrinkles on his forehead, or traces on his brain. His person is well turned, and of a good height. He is very ready at that sort of discourse with which men usually entertain women. He had all his life dressed very well, and remembers habits

as others do men. He can smile when one
speaks to him, and laughs easily. He knows
the history of every mode, and can inform
you from which of the French king's wenches,
our wives and daughters had their manner of
curling their hair, that way of placing their
hoods ; whose frailty was covered by such a
sort of petticoat, and whose vanity to show
her foot made that part of the dress so short
in such a year. In a word, all his conversation and knowledge has been in the female
world. As other men of his age will take
notice to you what such a minister said on
such and such an occasion, he will tell you,
when the duke of Monmouth danced at court,
such a woman was then smitten, another was
taken with him at the head of his troop in the
Park. In all these important relations, he
has ever about the same time received a kind
glance, or a blow of a fan from some celebrated
beauty, mother of the present lord Such-a-one.
If you speak of a young commoner, that said
a lively thing in the house, he starts up, " He
has good blood in his vein ; Tom Mirable
begot him ; the rogue cheated me in that
affair ; that young fellow's mother used me
more like a dog than any woman I ever made
advances to." This way of talking of his, very
much enlivens the conversation among us of a
more sedate turn, and I find there is not one of

the company, but myself, who rarely speak at all, but speaks of him as that sort of man, who is usually called a well-bred fine gentleman. To conclude his character, where women are not concerned, he is an honest worthy man.

I cannot tell whether I am to account him, whom I am next to speak of, as one of our company ; for he visits us but seldom, but when he does, it adds to every man else a new enjoyment of himself. He is a clergyman, a very philosophic man, of general learning, great sanctity of life, and the most exact good breeding. He has the misfortune to be of a very weak constitution, and consequently cannot accept of such cares and business as preferments in his function would oblige him to ; he is therefore among divines what a chamber-counsellor is among lawyers. The probity of his mind, and the integrity of his life, create him followers, as being eloquent or loud advances others. He seldom introduces the subject he speaks upon ; but we are so far gone in years, that he observes when he is among us, an earnestness to have him fall on some topic divine, which he always treats with much authority, as one who has no interest in this world, as one who is hastening to the object of all his wishes, and conceives hope from his decays and infirmities. These are my ordinary companions.

R.

JOSEPH ADDISON

[1672–1719]

SIR ROGER AT CHURCH

" First, in obedience to thy country's rites,
Worship th' immortal gods."

I AM always very well pleased with a
country Sunday, and think, if keeping
holy the seventh day were only a
human institution, it would be the best method
that could have been thought of for the polish-
ing and civilizing of mankind. It is certain
the country people would soon degenerate
into a kind of savages and barbarians, were
there not such frequent returns of a stated
time, in which the whole village meet together
with their best faces, and in their cleanliest
habits, to converse with one another upon
indifferent subjects, hear their duties explained
to them, and join together in adoration of
the Supreme Being. Sunday clears away the
rust of the whole week, not only as it refreshes
in their minds the notions of religion, but as
it puts both the sexes upon appearing in their

most agreeable forms, and exerting all such qualities as are apt to give them a figure in the eye of the village. A country fellow distinguishes himself as much in the church-yard, as a citizen does upon the Change, the whole parish-politics being generally discussed in that place either after sermon or before the bell rings.

My friend Sir Roger, being a good church-man, has beautified the inside of his church with several texts of his own choosing. He has likewise given a handsome pulpit-cloth, and railed in the communion-table at his own expense. He has often told me, that at his coming to his estate he found his parishioners very irregular; and that in order to make them kneel and join in the responses, he gave every one of them a hassock and a common-prayer-book: and at the same time employed an itinerant singing-master, who goes about the country for that purpose, to instruct them rightly in the tunes of the Psalms; upon which they now very much value themselves, and indeed outdo most of the country churches that I have ever heard.

As Sir Roger is landlord to the whole congregation, he keeps them in very good order and will suffer nobody to sleep in it besides himself; for if by chance he has been surprised into a short nap at sermon, upon recovering out of it he stands up and looks about him, and if he sees any body else nodding, either wakes them himself, or sends his servants to them. Several other of the old knight's particularities break out upon these occasions. Sometimes he will be lengthening out a verse in the singing Psalms, half a minute after the rest of the congregation have done with it ; sometimes when he is pleased with the matter of his devotion, he pronounces " Amen " three or four times to the same prayer ; and sometimes stands up when every body else is upon their knees, to count the congregation, or see if any of his tenants are missing.

I was yesterday very much surprised to hear my old friend, in the midst of the service calling out to one John Matthews to mind what he was about, and not disturb the congregation. This John Matthews it seems is remarkable for being an idle fellow, and at that time was kicking his heels for his diversion. This authority of the knight, though exerted in that odd manner, which accompanies him in all circumstances of life, has a very good effect upon the parish, who are not polite enough to see any thing ridiculous in his behaviour ; besides that the general good sense and worthiness of his character make his friends observe these little singularities as foils that rather set off than blemish his good qualities.

As soon as the sermon is finished, nobody presumes to stir till Sir Roger is gone out of the church. The knight walks down from his seat in the chancel between a double row of his tenants, that stand bowing to him on each side; and every now and then inquires how such a one's wife, or mother, or son, or father do, whom he does not see at church; which is understood as a secret reprimand to the person that is absent.

The chaplain has often told me, that upon a catechising day, when Sir Roger has been pleased with a boy that answers well, he has ordered a bible to be given him next day for his encouragement; and sometimes accompanies it with a flitch of bacon to his mother. Sir Roger has likewise added five pounds a year to the clerk's place; and that he may encourage the young fellows to make themselves perfect in the church-service, has promised upon the death of the present incumbent, who is very old, to bestow it according to merit.

The fair understanding between Sir Roger and his chaplain, and their mutual concurrence in doing good, is the more remarkable, because the very next village is famous for the differences and contentions that rise between the parson and the 'squire, who live in a perpetual state of war. The parson is always preaching at the 'squire; and the 'squire, to be revenged on the parson, never comes to church. The 'squire has made all his tenants atheists and tythe-stealers; while the parson instructs them every Sunday in the dignity of his order, and insinuates to them, in almost every sermon, that he is a better man than his patron. In short, matters are come to such an extremity, that the 'squire has not said his prayers either in public or private this half-year; and that the parson threatens him, if he does not mend his manners, to pray for him in the face of the whole congregation.

Feuds of this nature, though too frequent in the country, are very fatal to the ordinary people; who are so used to be dazzled with riches, that they pay as much deference to the understanding of a man of an estate, as of a man of learning; and are very hardly brought to regard any truth, how important soever it may be, that is preached to them, when they know there are several men of five hundred a year who do not believe it.

JOSEPH ADDISON

[1672–1719]

SIR ROGER AT THE THEATRE

" *Respicere exemplar vitæ morumque jubebo,*
Doctum imitatorem et veras hinc ducere voces."
HOR., Ars Poet., 327.

" *Keep Nature's great original in view,*
And thence the living images pursue."
FRANCIS.

MY friend Sir Roger de Coverley, when we last met together at the club, told me that he had a great mind to see the new tragedy with me, assuring me at the same time, that he had not been at a play these twenty years. " The last I saw," said Sir Roger, " was ' The Committee,' which I should not have gone to neither, had not I been told beforehand that it was a good church of England comedy." He then proceeded to inquire of me who this distrest mother was ; and upon hearing that she was Hector's widow, he told me that her husband was a brave man, and that when he was a school-boy he had read his life at the end of the dictionary. My friend asked me in the next place, if there would not be some danger in coming home late, in case the Mohocks should be abroad. "I assure you," says he, "I thought I had fallen into their hands last night; for I observed two or three lusty black men that followed me half way up Fleet-street, and mended their pace behind me, in proportion as I put on to get away from them. You must know," continued the knight with a smile, "I fancied they had a mind to hunt me; for I remember an honest gentleman in my neighbourhood, who was served such a trick in King Charles the Second's time, for which reason he has not ventured himself in town ever since. I might have shown them very good sport, had this been their design; for, as I am an old fox-hunter, I should have turned and dodged, and have played them a thousand tricks they had never seen in their lives before." Sir Roger added, that "if these gentlemen had any such intention, they did not succeed very well in it; for I threw them out," says he, "at the end of Norfolk-street, where I doubled the corner, and got shelter in my lodgings before they could imagine what was become of me. However," says the knight, "if Captain Sentry will make one with us to-morrow night, and you will both of you call upon me about four o'clock, that we may be at the house before it is full, I will have my own coach in readiness to attend you, for John tells me he has got the fore-wheels mended."

The captain, who did not fail to meet me there at the appointed hour, bid Sir Roger fear nothing, for that he had put on the same sword which he made use of at the battle of Steenkirk. Sir Roger's servants, and among the rest my old friend the butler, had, I found, provided themselves with good oaken plants, to attend their master upon this occasion. When we had placed him in his coach, with myself at his left-hand, the captain before him, and his butler at the head of his footmen in the rear, we convoyed him in safety to the playhouse, where, after having marched up the entry in good order, the captain and I went in with him, and seated him betwixt us in the pit. As soon as the house was full, and the candles lighted, my old friend stood up, and looked about him with that pleasure which a mind seasoned with humanity naturally feels in itself, at the sight of a multitude of people who seem pleased with one another, and partake of the same common entertainment. I could not but fancy to myself, as the old man stood up in the middle of the pit, that he made a very proper centre to a tragic audience. Upon the entering of

Pyrrhus, the knight told me, that he did not
believe the king of France himself had a better
strut. I was indeed very attentive to my old
friend's remarks, because I looked upon them
as a piece of natural criticism, and was well
pleased to hear him, at the conclusion of
almost every scene, telling me that he could
not imagine how the play would end. One
while he appeared much concerned for Andromache ; and a little while after as much for
Hermione ; and was extremely puzzled to
think what would become of Pyrrhus.

When Sir Roger saw Andromache's obsti-
nate refusal to her lover's importunities, he
whispered me in the ear, that he was sure she
would never have him ; to which he added,
with a more than ordinary vehemence, " You
can't imagine, sir, what it is to have to do
with a widow." Upon Pyrrhus's threatening
afterwards to leave her, the knight shook his
head, and muttered to himself, " Ay, do if
you can." This part dwelt so much upon my
friend's imagination, that at the close of the
third act, as I was thinking of something else,
he whispered me in my ear, " These widows,
sir, are the most perverse creatures in the
world. But pray," says he, " you that are a
critic, is the play according to your dramatic
rules, as you call them ? Should your people
in tragedy always talk to be understood ?

SIR ROGER AT THE THEATRE

Why, there is not a single sentence in this play that I do not know the meaning of."

The fourth act very luckily began before I had time to give the old gentleman an answer. " Well," says the knight, sitting down with great satisfaction, " I suppose we are now to see Hector's ghost." He then renewed his attention, and, from time to time, fell a-praising the widow. He made, indeed, a little mistake as to one of her pages, whom at his first entering he took for Astyanax ; but quickly set himself right in that particular, though, at the same time, he owned he should have been very glad to have seen the little boy, who, says he, must needs be a very fine child by the account that is given of him. Upon Hermione's going off with a menace to Pyrrhus, the audience gave a loud clap, to which Sir Roger added, "On my word, a notable young baggage."

As there was a very remarkable silence and stillness in the audience during the whole action, it was natural for them to take the opportunity of the intervals between the acts to express their opinion of the players, and of their respective parts. Sir Roger, hearing a cluster of them praise Orestes, struck in with them, and told them, that he thought his friend Pylades was a very sensible man. As they were afterwards applauding Pyrrhus, Sir Roger put in a second time. " And let me tell you," says he, " though he speaks but little, I like the old fellow in whiskers as well as any of them." Captain Sentry, seeing two or three wags who sat near us lean with an attentive ear towards Sir Roger, and fearing lest they should smoke the knight, plucked him by the elbow, and whispered something in his ear, that lasted till the opening of the fifth act. The knight was wonderfully attentive to the account which Orestes gives of Pyrrhus's death, and at the conclusion of it, told me it was such a bloody piece of work, that he was glad it was not done upon the stage. Seeing afterwards Orestes in his raving fit, he grew more than ordinarily serious, and took occasion to moralize (in his way) upon an evil conscience, adding, that Orestes, in his madness, looked as if he saw something.

As we were the first that came into the house, so we were the last that went out of it ; being resolved to have a clear passage for our old friend, whom we did not care to venture among the jostling of the crowd. Sir Roger went out fully satisfied with his entertainment, and we guarded him to his lodging in the same manner that we brought him to the playhouse ; being highly pleased for my own part, not only with the performance of the 'excellent piece which had been presented, but with the satisfaction which it had given to the old man.

JOSEPH ADDISON
[1672–1719]

DEATH OF SIR ROGER DE COVERLEY

" Heu pieras ! heu prisca fides ! "
VIRG., Æn., vi, 878.

" Mirror of ancient faith !
Undaunted worth ! Inviolable truth ! "
DRYDEN.

WE last night received a piece of ill news at our club, which very sensibly afflicted every one of us. I question not but my readers themselves will be troubled at the hearing of it. To keep them no longer in suspense, Sir Roger de Coverley is dead. He departed this life at his house in the country, after a few weeks' sickness. Sir Andrew Freeport has a letter from one of his correspondents in those parts, that informs him the old man caught a cold at the county-sessions, as he was very warmly promoting an address of his own penning, in which he succeeded according to his wishes. But this particular comes from a whig justice of peace, who was always sir Roger's enemy and antagonist. I have letters both from the chaplain and captain Sentry, which mention nothing of it, but are filled with many particulars to the honour of the good old man. I have likewise a letter from the butler, who took so much care of me last summer when I was at the knight's house. As my friend the butler mentions, in the simplicity of his heart, several circumstances the others have passed over in silence, I shall give my reader a copy of his letter, without any alteration or diminution.

"HONOURED SIR,
"Knowing that you was my old master's good friend, I could not forbear sending you the melancholy news of his death, which has afflicted the whole country, as well as his poor servants, who loved him, I may say, better than we did our lives. I am afraid he caught his death the last county-sessions, where he would go to see justice done to a poor widow woman, and her fatherless children, that had been wronged by a neighbouring gentleman ; for you know, sir, my good master was always the poor man's friend. Upon his coming home, the first complaint he made was, that he had lost his roast-beef stomach, not being able to touch a sirloin, which was served up according to custom ; and you know he used to take great delight in it. From that time

forward he grew worse and worse, but still
kept a good heart to the last.   Indeed we were
once in great hope of his recovery, upon a
kind message that was sent him from the
widow lady whom he had made love to the
forty last years of his life ; but this only
proved a lightning before death.   He has
bequeathed to this lady, as a token of his love,
a great pearl necklace, and a couple of silver
bracelets set with jewels, which belonged to my
good old lady his mother.   He has bequeathed
the fine white gelding that he used to ride a
hunting upon to his chaplain, because he
thought he would be kind to him ; and has
left you all his books.   He has, moreover,
bequeathed to the chaplain a very pretty
tenement with good lands about it.   It being
a very cold day when he made his will, he left
for mourning to every man in the parish, a
great frieze-coat, and to every woman a black
riding-hood.   It was a moving sight to see him
take leave of his poor servants, commending
us all for our fidelity, whilst we were not able
to speak a word for weeping.   As we most of
us are grown gray-headed in our dear master's
service, he has left us pensions and legacies,
which we may live very comfortably upon the
remaining part of our days.   He has bequeathed a great deal more in charity, which
is not yet come to my knowledge, and it is

peremptorily said in the parish, that he has left money to build a steeple to the church ; for he was heard to say some time ago, that, if he lived two years longer, Coverley church should have a steeple to it. The chaplain tells every body that he made a very good end, and never speaks of him without tears. He was buried, according to his own directions, among the family of the Coverleys, on the left hand of his father, Sir Arthur. The coffin was carried by six of his tenants, and the pall held up by six of the quorum. The whole parish followed the corpse with heavy hearts, and in their mourning suits ; the men in frieze, and the women in riding-hoods. Captain Sentry, my master's nephew, has taken possession of the Hall-house, and the whole estate. When my old master saw him, a little before his death, he shook him by the hand, and wished him joy of the estate which was falling to him, desiring him only to make a good use of it, and to pay the several legacies, and the gifts of charity, which he told him he had left as quit-rents upon the estate. The captain truly seems a courteous man, though he says but little. He makes much of those whom my master loved, and shows great kindness to the old house-dog, that you know my poor master was so fond of. It would have gone to your heart to have heard the moans the dumb creature made on the day of my master's death. He has never joyed himself since ; no more has any of us. It was the melancholiest day for the poor people that ever happened in Worcestershire. This being all from,

"Honoured Sir,

"Your most sorrowful servant,

"EDWARD BISCUIT.

"P.S. My master desired, some weeks before he died, that a book, which comes up to you by the carrier, should be given to Sir Andrew Freeport in his name."

This letter, notwithstanding the poor butler's manner of writing it, gave us such an idea of our good old friend, that upon the reading of it there was not a dry eye in the club.

Sir Andrew, opening the book, found it to be a collection of acts of parliament. There was in particular the Act of Uniformity, with some passages in it marked by Sir Roger's own hand. Sir Andrew found that they related to two or three points which he had disputed with Sir Roger, the last time he appeared at the club. Sir Andrew, who would have been merry at such an incident on another occasion, at the sight of the old man's writing burst into tears, and put the book in his pocket. Captain Sentry informs me that the knight has left ring, and mourning for every one in the club.

JONATHAN SWIFT

[1667–1745]

A COUNTRY VISIT

" . . . *Ingenuas didicisse fideliter artes*
Emollit mores. . . ."

OVID.

From my own apartment in Channel-row,
March 5

THOSE inferior duties of life, which the
French call *Les petites morales*, or the
smaller morals, are with us distinguished by the name of good manners
or breeding. This I look upon, in the general
notion of it, to be a sort of artificial good
sense, adapted to the meanest capacities, and
introduced to make mankind easy in their
commerce with each other. Low and little
understandings, without some rules of this
kind, would be perpetually wandering into
a thousand indecencies and irregularities in
behaviour ; and in their ordinary conversation
fall into the same boisterous familiarities,
that one observes amongst them, when

74

a debauch hath quite taken away the
use of their reason. In other instances it
is odd to consider, that for want of common discretion, the very end of good
breeding is wholly perverted, and civility,
intended to make us easy, is employed in
laying chains and fetters upon us, in debarring
us of our wishes, and in crossing our most
reasonable desires and inclinations. This
abuse reigns chiefly in the country, as I found
to my vexation when I was last there, in a
visit I made to a neighbour about two miles
from my cousin. As soon as I entered the
parlour, they put me into the great chair that
stood close by a huge fire, and kept me there
by force until I was almost stifled. Then a
boy came in a great hurry to pull off my boots,
which I in vain opposed, urging that I must
return soon after dinner. In the mean time,
the good lady whispered her eldest daughter,
and slipped a key into her hand; the girl
returned instantly with a beer-glass half full
of *acqua mirabilis* and syrup of gillyflowers. I
took as much as I had a mind for, but Madam
vowed I should drink it off; for she was sure
it would do me good after coming out of the
cold air; and I was forced to obey, which
absolutely took away my stomach. When
dinner came in, I had a mind to sit at a distance
from the fire; but they told me it was as

much as my life was worth, and set me with my back just against it. Although my appetite was quite gone, I was resolved to force down as much as I could, and desired the leg of a pullet. "Indeed, Mr. Bickerstaff," says the Lady, "you must eat a wing to oblige me," and so put a couple upon my plate. I was persecuted at this rate during the whole meal; as often as I called for small beer, the master tipped the wink, and the servant brought me a brimmer of October. Some time after dinner I ordered my cousin's man, who came with me, to get ready the horses; but it was resolved that I should not stir that night; and when I seemed pretty much bent upon going, they ordered the stable door to be locked, and the children hid my cloak and boots. The next question was, what would I have for supper? I said, I never eat any thing at night: but was at last, in my own defence, obliged to name the first thing that came into my head. After three hours spent chiefly in apologies for my entertainment, insinuating to me, "That this was "the worst time of the year for provisions, "that they were at a great distance from any "market; that they were afraid I should be "starved; and that they knew they kept me "to my loss"; the Lady went, and left me to her husband; for they took special care I should never be alone : as soon as her back was turned, the little misses ran backwards and forwards, every moment, and constantly as they came in or went out made a curtsey directly at me, which, in good manners, I was forced to return with a bow, and *your humble servant, pretty Miss.* Exactly at eight, the mother came up, and discovered, by the redness of her face, that supper was not far off. It was twice as large as the dinner, and my persecution doubled in proportion. I desired, at my usual hour, to go to my repose, and was conducted to my chamber by the gentleman, his lady, and the whole train of children. They importuned me to drink something before I went to bed ; and, upon my refusing, at last left a bottle of *stingo*, as they called it, for fear I should wake and be thirsty in the night. I was forced in the morning to rise and dress myself in the dark, because they would not suffer my kinsman's servant to disturb me at the hour I desired to be called. I was now resolved to break through all measures to get away ; and, after sitting down to a monstrous breakfast of cold beef, mutton, neats tongues, venison pasty, and stale beer, took leave of the family. But the gentleman would needs see me part of the way, and carry me a short cut through his own ground, which he told me would save half a mile's riding. This last piece of civility had like to have cost me dear, being once or twice in danger of my neck by leaping over his ditches, and at last forced to alight in the dirt, when my horse having slipped his bridle ran away, and took us up more than an hour to recover him again.

It is evident, that none of the absurdities I met with in this visit proceeded from an ill intention, but from a wrong judgment of complaisance, and a misapplication in the rules of it. I cannot so easily excuse the more refined critics upon behaviour, who, having professed no other study, are yet infinitely defective in the most material parts of it. Ned Fashion hath been bred all his life about court, and understands to a tittle all the punctilios of a drawing room. He visits most of the fine women near St. James's, and upon every occasion says the civilest and softest things to them of any man breathing. To Mr. Isaac he owes an easy slide in his bow, and a graceful manner of coming into a room : but in some other cases he is very far from being a well bred person. He laughs at men of far superior understanding to his own, for not being as well dressed as himself; despiseth all his acquaintance who are not of quality, and in public places hath on that account often avoided taking notice of some among the best speakers of the house of commons. He raileth strenuously at both universities before the members of either ; and is never heard to swear an oath, or break in upon religion and morality, except in the company of divines. On the other hand, a man of right sense hath all the essentials of good breeding, although he may be wanting in the forms of it. Horatio hath spent most of his time at Oxford : he hath a great deal of learning, an agreeable wit, and as much modesty as may serve to adorn without concealing his other good qualities. In that retired way of living he seemeth to have formed a notion of human nature, as he hath found it described in the writings of the greatest men, not as he is likely to meet with it in the common course of life. Hence it is, that he giveth no offence, but converseth with great deference, candor, and humanity. His bow, I must confess, is somewhat awkward ; but then he hath an extensive, universal, and unaffected knowledge, which may perhaps a little excuse him. He would make no extra-ordinary figure at a ball ; but I can assure the ladies in his behalf, and for their own consolation, that he has writ better verses on the sex than any man now living, and is preparing such a poem for the press as will transmit their praises and his own to many generations.

JONATHAN SWIFT

[1667–1745]

A MEDITATION UPON A BROOMSTICK

According to the style and manner of the Honourable ROBERT BOYLE'S Meditations.

THIS single stick, which you now behold ingloriously lying in that neglected corner, I once knew in a flourishing state in a forest: it was full of sap, full of leaves, and full of boughs: but now, in vain does the busy art of man pretend to vye with nature, by tying that withered bundle of twigs to its sapless trunk: it is now at best but the reverse of what it was; a tree turned upside down, the branches on the earth, and the root in the air: it is now handled by every dirty wench, condemned to do her drudgery: and by a capricious kind of fate, destined to make other things clean, and be nasty itself. At length, worn to the stumps in the service of the maids, it is either thrown out of doors, or condemned to the last use of kindling a fire. When I beheld this, I sighed, and said within myself,

A MEDITATION UPON A BROOMSTICK

SURELY MORTAL MAN IS A BROOMSTICK ! Nature sent him into the world strong and lusty, in a thriving condition, wearing his own hair on his head, the proper branches of this reasoning vegetable ; until the ax of intemperance has lopped off his green boughs, and left him a withered trunk : he then flies to art, and puts on a *periwig* ; valuing himself upon an unnatural bundle of hairs, covered with powder, that never grew on his head : but now should this our *broomstick* pretend to enter the scene, proud of those *birchen* spoils it never bore, and all covered with dust, though the sweepings of the finest lady's chamber ; we should be apt to ridicule and despise its vanity. Partial judges that we are of our own excellences, and other men's defaults !

But a *broomstick*, perhaps, you will say, is an emblem of a tree, standing on its head ; and pray what is man but a topsy-turvy creature ? his animal faculties perpetually mounted on his rational, his head where his heels should be, grovelling on the earth. And yet, with all his faults, he sets up to be an universal reformer and corrector of abuses ; a remover of grievances ; rakes unto every slut's corner of nature, bringing hidden corruptions to the light, and raises a mighty dust where there was none before ; sharing deeply

F   81

all the while in the very same pollutions he pretended to sweep away. His last days are spent in slavery to women, and generally the least deserving ; till worn to the stumps, like his brother *besom*, he is either kicked out of doors, or made use of to kindle flames for others to warm themselves by.

SAMUEL JOHNSON

[1709–1784]

A JOURNEY IN A STAGE COACH

" . . . *Tolle periculum,*
Jam vaga prosiliet frœnis natura remotis."

HOR.

" *But take the danger and the shame away,*
And vagrant nature bounds upon her prey."

FRANCIS.

To the Adventurer

SIR,

IT has been observed, I think, by Sir William Temple, and after him by almost every other writer, that England affords a greater variety of characters than the rest of the world. This is ascribed to the liberty prevailing amongst us, which gives every man the privilege of being wise or foolish his own way, and preserves him from the necessity of hypocrisy or the servility of imitation.

That the position itself is true, I am not completely satisfied. To be nearly acquainted with the people of different countries can

happen to very few ; and in life, as in everything else beheld at a distance, there appears
an even uniformity : the petty discriminations
which diversify the natural character, are not
discoverable but by a close inspection ; we,
therefore, find them most at home, because
there we have most opportunities of remarking
them. Much less am I convinced that this
peculiar diversification, if it be real, is the
consequence of peculiar liberty ; for where is
the government to be found that superintends
individuals with so much vigilance as not to
leave their private conduct without restraint ?
Can it enter into a reasonable mind to imagine,
that men of every other nation are not equally
masters of their own time or houses with ourselves, and equally at liberty to be parsi-
monious or profuse, frolic or sullen, abstinent
or luxurious ? Liberty is certainly necessary
to the full play of predominant humours ;
but such liberty is to be found alike under
the government of the many or the few, in
monarchies or in common-wealths.

How readily the predominant passion
snatches an interval of liberty, and how fast
it expands itself when the weight of restraint
is taken away, I had lately an opportunity to
discover, as I took a journey into the country
in a stage-coach ; which, as every journey is
a kind of adventure, may be very properly

related to you, though I can display no such
extraordinary assembly, as Cervantes has
collected at Don Quixote's inn.

In a stage-coach the passengers are for the
most part wholly unknown to one another,
and without expectation of ever meeting again
when their journey is at an end ; one should
therefore imagine, that it was of little importance to any of them what conjectures the
rest should form concerning him. Yet so it
is, that as all think themselves secure from
detection, all assume that character of which
they are most desirous, and on no occasion
is the general ambition of superiority more
apparently indulged.

On the day of our departure, in the twilight
of the morning, I ascended the vehicle with
three men and two women, my fellow-travellers.
It was easy to observe the affected elevation
of mien with which every one entered, and the
supercilious civility with which they paid their
compliments to each other. When the first
ceremony was despatched, we sat silent for a
long time, all employed in collecting importance
into our faces, and endeavouring to strike
reverence and submission into our companions.

It is always observable, that silence pro-
pagates itself, and that the longer talk has
been suspended, the more difficult it is to find
anything to say. We began now to wish for

conversation; but no one seemed inclined to descend from his dignity, or first to propose a topic of discourse. At last a corpulent gentleman, who had equipped himself for this expedition with a scarlet surtout and a large hat with a broad lace, drew out his watch, looked on it in silence, and then held it dangling at his finger. This was, I suppose, understood by all the company as an invitation to ask the time of day, but nobody appeared to heed his overture; and his desire to be talking so far overcame his resentment, that he let us know of his own accord that it was past five, and that in two hours we should be at breakfast.

His condescension was thrown away; we continued all obdurate; the ladies held up their heads; I amused myself with watching their behaviour; and of the other two, one seemed to employ himself in counting the trees as we drove by them, the other drew his hat over his eyes and counterfeited a slumber. The man of benevolence, to show that he was not depressed by our neglect, hummed a tune, and beat time upon his snuff-box.

Thus universally displeased with one another, and not much delighted with ourselves, we came at last to the little inn appointed for our repast; and all began at once to recompense themselves for the constraint of silence, by innumerable questions and orders to the people

that attended us. At last, what every one
had called for was got, or declared impossible
to be got at that time, and we were persuaded
to sit round the same table ; when the gentleman in the red surtout looked again upon his
watch, told us that we had half an hour to
spare, but he was sorry to see so little merriment among us ; that all fellow-travellers were
for the time upon the level, and that it was
always his way to make himself one of the
company. " I remember," says he, " it was
on just such a morning as this, that I and my
Lord Mumble and the Duke of Tenterden were
out upon a ramble : we called at a little house
as it might be this ; and my landlady, I
warrant you, not suspecting to whom she was
talking, was so jocular and facetious, and made
so many merry answers to our questions, that
we were all ready to burst with laughter. At
last the good woman happening to overhear
me whisper the duke, and call him by his title,
was so surprised and confounded that we could
scarcely get a word from her ; and the duke
never met me from that day to this, but he
talks of the little house, and quarrels with me
for terrifying the landlady.

He had scarcely time to congratulate himself
on the veneration which this narrative must
have procured him from the company, when
one of the ladies having reached out for a

plate on a distant part of the table, began to remark " the inconveniences of travelling and the difficulty which they who never sat at home without a great number of attendants found in performing for themselves such offices as the road required ; but that people of quality often travelled in disguise and might be generally known from the vulgar by their condescension to poor innkeepers, and the allowance which they made for any defect in their entertainment ; that for her part, while people were civil and meant well, it was never her custom to find fault, for one was not to expect upon a journey all that one enjoyed at one's own house."

A general emulation seemed now to be excited. One of the men, who had hitherto said nothing, called for the last newspaper ; and having perused it a while with deep pensiveness, " It is impossible," says he," for any man to guess how to act with regard to the stocks : last week it was the general opinion that they would fall ; and I sold out twenty thousand pounds in order to a purchase ; they have now risen unexpectedly ; and I make no doubt but at my return to London I shall risk thirty thousand pounds amongst them again."

A young man, who had hitherto distinguished himself only by the vivacity of his looks and a frequent diversion of his eyes from one object to another, upon this closed his snuff-box, and told us that " he had a hundred times talked with the chancellor and the judges on the subject of the stocks ; that, for his part, he did not pretend to be well acquainted with the principles upon which they were established, but had always heard them reckoned pernicious to trade, uncertain in their produce, and un-solid in their foundation ; and that he had been advised by three judges, his most intimate friends, never to venture his money in the funds, but to put it out upon land-security till he could light upon an estate in his own country."

It might be expected, that upon these glimpses of latent dignity, we should all have begun to look round us with veneration ; and have behaved like the princes of romance, when the enchantment that disguises them is dissolved, and they discover the dignity of each other : yet it happened, that none of these hints made much impression on the company ; every one was apparently suspected of endeavouring to impose false appearances upon the rest ; all continued their haughtiness in hopes to enforce their claims ; and all grew every hour more sullen because they found their representations of themselves without effect.

Thus we travelled on four days with male-

volence perpetually increasing, and without
any endeavour but to outvie each other in
superciliousness and neglect ; and when any
two of us could separate ourselves for a moment
we vented our indignation at the sauciness of
the rest.

At length the journey was at an end, and
time and chance, that strip off all disguises,
have discovered, that the intimate of lords and
dukes is a nobleman's butler, who has furnished
a shop with the money he has saved ; the man
who deals so largely in the funds, is a clerk
of a broker in 'Change-alley ; the lady who so
carefully concealed her quality, keeps a cook-
shop behind the Exchange ; and the young
man who is so happy in the friendship of the
judges, engrosses and transcribes for bread in
a garret of the temple. Of one of the women
only I could make no disadvantageous detection, because she had assumed no character,
but accommodated herself to the scene before
her, without any struggle for distinction or
superiority.

I could not forbear to reflect on the folly
of practising a fraud which, as the event
showed, had been already practised too often
to succeed, and by the success of which no
advantage could have been obtained ; of
assuming a character which was to end with
the day ; and of claiming upon false pretences

honours which must perish with the breath that paid them.

But, Mr. Adventurer, let not those who laugh at me and my companions think this folly confined to a stage-coach. Every man in the journey of life takes the same advantage of the ignorance of his fellow-travellers, disguises himself in counterfeited merit, and hears those praises with complacency which his conscience reproaches him for accepting. Every man deceives himself, while he thinks he is deceiving others, and forgets that the time is at hand when every illusion shall cease, when fictitious excellence shall be torn away, and all must be shown to all in their real state.

I am, Sir,

Your humble servant,

VIATOR.

OLIVER GOLDSMITH

[1728–1774]

BEAU TIBBS (1)

THOUGH naturally pensive, yet I am fond of gay company, and take every opportunity of thus dismissing the mind from duty. From this motive I am often found in the centre of a crowd, and wherever pleasure is to be sold am always a purchaser. In those places, without being remarked by any, I join in whatever goes forward, work my passion into a similitude of frivolous earnestness, shout as they shout, and condemn as they happen to disapprove. A mind thus sunk for a while below its natural standard is qualified for stronger flights, as those first retire who would spring forward with greater vigour.

Attracted by the serenity of the evening, my friend and I lately went to gaze upon the company in one of the public walks near the city. Here we sauntered together for some time, either praising the beauty of such as

were handsome, or the dresses of such as had
nothing else to recommend them. We had
gone thus deliberately forward for some time,
when, stopping on a sudden, my friend caught
me by the elbow and led me out of the public
walk; I could perceive by the quickness of
his pace and by his frequently looking behind
that he was attempting to avoid somebody
who followed. We now turned to the right,
then to the left. As we went forward he still
went faster, but in vain; the person whom
he attempted to escape hunted us through
every doubling, and gained upon us each
moment, so that at last we fairly stood still,
resolving to face what we could not avoid.

Our pursuer soon came up, and joined us
with all the familiarity of an old acquaintance.
" My dear Drybone," cries he, shaking my
friend's hand, "where have you been hiding
this half a century ? Positively I had fancied
you were gone down to cultivate matrimony
and your estate in the country." During the
reply I had an opportunity of surveying the
appearance of our new companion; his hat
was pinched up with peculiar smartness; his
looks were pale, thin, and sharp; round his
neck he wore a broad black ribbon, and in his
bosom a buckle studded with glass; his coat
was trimmed with tarnished twist; he wore
by his side a sword with a black hilt; and his

stockings of silk, though newly washed, were grown yellow by long service. I was so much engaged with the peculiarity of his dress that I attended only to the latter part of my friend's reply, in which he complimented Mr. Tibbs on the taste of his clothes, and the bloom in his countenance. "Psha, psha, Will!" cried the figure; "no more of that if you love me; you know I hate flattery—on my soul I do; and yet, to be sure, an intimacy with the great will improve one's appearance, and a course of venison will fatten; and yet, faith, I despise the great as much as you do. But there are a great many damn'd honest fellows among them, and we must not quarrel with one half because the other wants weeding. If they were all such as my Lord Mudler, one of the most good-natured creatures that ever squeezed a lemon, I should myself be among the number of their admirers. I was yesterday to dine at the Duchess of Piccadilly's; my lord was there. 'Ned,' says he to me, 'Ned,' says he, 'I will hold gold to silver I can tell where you were poaching last night.' 'Poaching, my lord?' says I; 'faith, you have missed already, for I stayed at home and let the girls poach for me. That's my way; I take a fine woman as some animals do their prey; stand still and swoop; they fall into my mouth.'"

BEAU TIBBS (1)

" Ah, Tibbs, thou art an happy fellow," cried my companion, with looks of infinite pity ; " I hope your fortune is as much improved as your understanding in such company." " Improved," replied the other ; " you know—— But let it go no farther—a great secret—five hundred a year to begin with—my lord's word of honour for it. His lordship took me down in his own chariot yesterday, and we had a *tête-à-tête* dinner in the country, where we talked of nothing else." " I fancy you forgot, sir," cried I, " you told us but this moment of your dining yesterday in town." " Did I say so ? " replied he coolly ; " to be sure, if I said so it was so. Dined in town ? Egad, now I do remember, I did dine in town ; but I dined in the country too, for you must know, my boys, I eat two dinners. By-the-bye, I am grown as nice as the devil in my eating. I will tell you a pleasant affair about that : we were a select party of us to dine at Lady Grogram's, an affected piece—— But let it go no further —a secret ; well, there happened to be no assafœtida in the sauce to a turkey, upon which, says I, I will hold a thousand guineas and say done first that—— But, dear Dry-bone, you are an honest creature, lend me half-a-crown for a minute or two or so, just till—— But, harkee, ask me for it the next time we meet, or it may be twenty to one but I forget to pay you."

OLIVER GOLDSMITH

When he left us our conversation naturally turned upon so extraordinary a character. "His very dress," cries my friend, "is not less extraordinary than his conduct. If you meet him this day you find him in rags, if the next in embroidery. With those persons of distinction of whom he talks so familiarly, he has scarce a coffee-house acquaintance. However, both for interests of society and perhaps for his own, Heaven has made him poor, and while all the world perceive his wants, he fancies them concealed from every eye. An agreeable companion because he understands flattery; and all must be pleased with the first part of his conversation, though all are sure of its ending with a demand on their purse. While his youth countenances the levity of his conduct, he may thus earn a precarious subsistence, but when age comes on, the gravity of which is incompatible with buffoonery, then will he find himself forsaken by all, condemned in the decline of life to hang upon some rich family whom he once despised, there to undergo all the ingenuity of studied contempt, to be employed only as a spy upon the servants, or a bugbear to fright the children into obedience."

OLIVER GOLDSMITH

[1728–1774]

BEAU TIBBS (2)

I AM apt to fancy I have contracted a new acquaintance, whom it will be no easy matter to shake off. My little beau yesterday overtook me again in one of the public walks, and slapping me on the shoulder saluted me with an air of the most perfect familiarity. His dress was the same as usual, except that he had more powder in his hair, wore a dirtier shirt, a pair o temple spectacles, and his hat under his arm.

As I knew him to be an harmless, amusing little thing, I could not return his smiles with any degree of severity ; so we walked forward on terms of the utmost intimacy, and in a few minutes discussed all the usual topics preliminary to particular conversation.

The oddities that marked his character, however, soon began to appear ; he bowed to several well-dressed persons, who, by their manner of returning the compliment, appeared perfect strangers. At intervals he drew out a

pocket-book, seeming to take memorandums
before all the company, with much importance
and assiduity. In this manner he led me
through the length of the whole walk, fretting
at his absurdities, and fancying myself laughed
at not less than him by every spectator.

When we got to the end of our procession,
" Bless me," cries he, with an air of vivacity,
" I never saw the park so thin in my life
before ; there's no company at all to-day—
not a single face to be seen." "No company ?"
interrupted I peevishly ; " no company where
there is such a crowd ? Why, man, there's
too much. What are the thousands that have
been laughing at us but company ?" "Lord,
my dear," returned he, with the utmost good
humour, " you seem immensely chagrined ;
but, blast me, when the world laughs at me,
I laugh at the world, and so we are even. My
Lord Trip, Bill Squash the Creolian, and I
sometimes make a party at being ridiculous,
and so we say and do a thousand things for the
joke sake. But I see you are grave, and if you
are for a fine, grave, sentimental companion, you
shall dine with me and my wife to-day ; I must
insist on't. I will introduce you to Mrs. Tibbs,
a lady of as elegant qualifications as any in
Nature ; she was bred—but that's between ourselves—under the inspection of the Countess of
Allnight. A charming body of voice—— But

no more of that; she will give us a song. You
shall see my little girl, too, Carolina Wilhelmina
Amelia Tibbs, a sweet, pretty creature; I design
her for my Lord Drumstick's eldest son ; but
that's in friendship, let it go no farther ; she's
but six years old, and yet she walks a minuet,
and plays on the guitar immensely already.
I intend she shall be as perfect as possible in
every accomplishment. In the first place, I
will make her a scholar ; I'll teach her Greek
myself, and learn that language purposely to
instruct her—but let that be a secret."

Thus saying, without waiting for a reply, he
took me by the arm and hauled me along. We
passed through many dark alleys and winding
ways, for, from some motives to me unknown,
he seemed to have a particular aversion to
every frequented street. At last, however we
got to the door of a dismal-looking house in
the outlets of the town, where, he informed
me, he chose to reside for the benefit of the air.

We entered the lower door, which ever seemed
to lie most hospitably open, and I began to
ascend an old and creaking staircase, when, as
he mounted to show me the way, he demanded
whether I delighted in prospects ; to which
answering in the affirmative, " Then," says he,
" I shall show you one of the most charming in
the world out of my windows ; we shall see the
ships sailing and the whole country for twenty

miles round, tip-top, quite high. My Lord Swamp would give ten thousand guineas for such a one, but as I sometimes pleasantly tell him, I always love to keep my prospects at home, that my friends may see me the oftener."

By this time we were arrived as high as the stairs would permit us to ascend, till we came to what he facetiously pleased to call the first floor down the chimney, and, knocking at the door, a voice from within demanded, "Who's there?" My conductor answered that it was he. But this not satisfying the querist, the voice again repeated the demand, to which he answered louder than before, and now the door was opened by an old woman with cautious reluctance.

When we got in he welcomed me to his house with great ceremony, and, turning to the old woman, asked where was her lady. "Good troth," replied she in a peculiar dialect, "she's washing your two shirts at the next door, because they have taken an oath against lending out the tub any longer." "My two shirts?" cries he in a tone that faltered with confusion, "what does the idiot mean?" "I ken what I mean well enough," replied the other; "she's washing your two shirts at the next door, because——" "Fire and fury, no more of thy stupid explanations!" cried he; "go and inform her we have got company. Were that Scotch hag to be for ever in my

family, she would never learn politeness, nor
forget that absurd, poisonous accent of hers,
or testify the smallest specimen of breeding or
high life ; and yet it is very surprising, too,
as I had her from a parliament man, a friend
of mine, from the Highlands, one of the
politest men in the world ; but that's a secret."

We waited some time for Mrs. Tibbs' arrival,
during which interval I had a full opportunity
of surveying the chamber and all its furniture ;
which consisted of four chairs with old wrought
bottoms, that he assured me were his wife's
embroidery, a square table that had been
once japanned, a cradle in one corner, a
lumbering cabinet in the other ; a broken
shepherdess and a mandarin without a head
were stuck over the chimney, and round the
walls several paltry unframed pictures, which,
he observed, were all his own drawing. "What
do you think, sir, of that head in the corner, done
in the manner of Grisoni ? There's the true keeping in it ; it's my own face, and though there
happens to be no likeness, a Countess offered me
a hundred for its fellow. I refused her, for, hang
it, that would be mechanical, you know ! "

The wife at last made her appearance, at once
a slattern and a coquette, much emaciated, but
still carrying the remains of beauty. She made
twenty apologies for being seen in such an odious
dishabille, but hoped to be excused, as she had

stayed out all night at the gardens with the
Countess, who was excessively fond of the horns.
"And, indeed, my dear," added she, turning to
her husband, " his lordship drank your health in
a bumper." " Poor Jack," cries he, " a dear
good-natured creature ; I know he loves me.
But I hope, my dear, you have given orders for
dinner; you need make no great preparations,
neither, there are but three of us ; something
elegant, and little will do—a turbot, an ortolan,
or a——" "Or what do you think, my dear,"
interrupts the wife, " of a nice pretty bit of ox-
cheek, piping hot, and dressed with a little of my
own sauce ? " " The very thing," replies he; " it
will eat best with some smart bottled beer; but be
sure to let's have the sauce his grace was so fond
of. I hate your immense loads of meat—that is
country all over ; extreme disgusting to those
who are in the least acquainted with high life."

By this time my curiosity began to abate,
and my appetite to increase ; the company of
fools may at first make us smile, but at last
never fails of rendering us melancholy. I
therefore pretended to recollect a prior engage-
ment, and after having shown my respect to
the house, according to the fashion of the
English, by giving the old servant a piece of
money at the door, I took my leave, Mr.
Tibbs assuring me that dinner, if I stayed,
would be ready at least in less than two hours.

CHARLES LAMB

[1775–1834]

I HAVE an almost feminine partiality for old china. When I go to see any great house, I enquire for the china-closet, and next for the picture gallery. I cannot defend the order of preference, but by saying, that we have all some taste or other, of too ancient a date to admit of our remembering distinctly that it was an acquired one. I can call to mind the first play, and the first exhibition, that I was taken to ; but I am not conscious of a time when china jars and saucers were introduced into my imagination.

I had no repugnance then—why should I now have ?—to those little, lawless, azure-tinctured grotesques, that under the notion of men and women, float about, uncircumscribed by any element, in that world before perspective—a china tea-cup.

I like to see my old friends—whom distance cannot diminish—figuring up in the air (so

they appear to our optics), yet on *terra firma*
still—for so we must in courtesy interpret
that speck of deeper blue,—which the decorous
artist, to prevent absurdity, had made to
spring up beneath their sandals.

I love the men with women's faces, and the
women, if possible, with still more womanish
expressions.

Here is a young and courtly Mandarin,
handing tea to a lady from a salver—two
miles off. See how distance seems to set off
respect ! And here the same lady, or another
—for likeness is identity on tea-cups—is stepping into a little fairy boat, moored on the
higher side of this calm garden river, with a
dainty mincing foot, which in a right angle
of incidence (as angles go in our world) must
infallibly land her in the midst of a flowery
mead—a furlong off on the other side of the
same strange stream !

Farther on—if far or near can be predicated
of their world—see horses, trees, pagodas,
dancing the hays.

Here—a cow and rabbit couchant, and
co-extensive—so objects show, seen through
the lucid atmosphere of fine Cathay.

I was pointing out to my cousin last evening,
over our Hyson, (which we are old fashioned
enough to drink unmixed still of an afternoon)
some of those *speciosa miracula* upon a set of

extraordinary old blue china (a recent purchase) which we were now for the first time using ; and could not help remarking, how favourable circumstances had been to us of late years, that we could afford to please the eye sometimes with trifles of this sort—when a passing sentiment seemed to overshade the brows of my companion. I am quick at detecting these summer clouds in Bridget.

" I wish the good old times would come again," she said, " when we were not quite so rich. I do not mean, that I want to be poor ; but there was a middle state "—so she was pleased to ramble on,—" in which I am sure we were a great deal happier. A purchase is but a purchase, now that you have money enough and to spare. Formerly it used to be a triumph. When we coveted a cheap luxury (and, O ! how much ado I had to get you to consent in those times !)—we were used to have a debate two or three days before, and to weigh the *for* and *against*, and think what we might spare it out of, and what saving we could hit upon, that should be an equivalent. A thing was worth buying then, when we felt the money that we paid for it.

" Do you remember the brown suit, which you made to hang upon you, till all your friends cried shame upon you, it grew so thread-bare—and all because of that folio

Beaumont and Fletcher, which you dragged
home late at night from Barker's in Covent
Garden ? Do you remember how we eyed it
for weeks before we could make up our minds
to the purchase, and had not come to a
determination till it was near ten o'clock of
the Saturday night, when you set off from
Islington, fearing you should be too late—
and when the old bookseller with some
grumbling opened his shop, and by the
twinkling taper (for he was setting bedwards)
lighted out the relic from his dusty treasures
—and when you lugged it home, wishing it
were twice as cumbersome—and when you
presented it to me—and when we were explor-
ing the perfectness of it (*collating* you called it)
—and while I was repairing some of the loose
leaves with paste, which your impatience
would not suffer to be left till daybreak—was
there no pleasure in being a poor man ? or can
those neat black clothes which you wear now,
and are so careful to keep brushed, since we
have become rich and finical, give you half
the honest vanity, with which you flaunted it
about in that overworn suit—your old corbeau
—for four or five weeks longer than you should
have done, to pacify your conscience for the
mighty sum of fifteen—or sixteen shillings
was it ?—a great affair we thought it then—
which you had lavished on the old folio. Now

you can afford to buy any book that pleases you, but I do not see that you ever bring me home any nice old purchases now.

" When you came home with twenty apologies for laying out a less number of shillings upon that print after Lionardo, which we christened the ' Lady Blanch ' ; when you looked at the purchase, and thought of the money—and thought of the money, and looked again at the picture—was there no pleasure in being a poor man ? Now, you have nothing to do but to walk into Colnaghi's and buy a wilderness of Lionardos. Yet do you ?

" Then, do you remember our pleasant walks to Enfield, and Potter's Bar, and Waltham, when we had a holyday—holydays, and all other fun, are gone, now we are rich—and the little hand-basket in which I used to deposit our day's fare of savoury cold lamb and salad —and how you would pry about at noon-tide for some decent house, where we might go in, and produce our store—only paying for the ale that you must call for—and speculate upon the looks of the landlady, and whether she was likely to allow us a table-cloth—and wish for such another honest hostess, as Izaac Walton has described many a one on the pleasant banks of the Lea, when he went a fishing—and sometimes they would prove obliging enough, and sometimes they would look grudgingly upon us

—but we had cheerful looks still for one another, and would eat our plain food savorily, scarcely grudging Piscator his Trout Hall ? Now,—when we go out a day's pleasuring, which is seldom moreover, we *ride* part of the way—and go into a fine inn, and order the best of dinners, never debating the expense—which, after all, never has half the relish of those chance country snaps, when we were at the mercy of uncertain usage, and a precarious welcome.

" You are too proud to see a play anywhere now but in the pit. Do you remember where it was we used to sit, when we saw the Battle of Hexham, and the Surrender of Calais, and Bannister and Mrs. Bland in the Children in the Wood—when we squeezed out our shillings a-piece to sit three or four times in a season in the one-shilling gallery—where you felt all the time that you ought not to have brought me—and more strongly I felt obligation to you for having brought me—and the pleasure was the better for a little shame—and when the curtain drew up, what cared we for our place in the house, or what mattered it where we were sitting, when our thoughts were with Rosalind in Arden, or with Viola at the Court of Illyria ? You used to say, that the Gallery was the best place of all for enjoying a play socially—that the relish of such exhibitions must be in proportion to the

infrequency of going—that the company we
met there, not being in general readers of
plays, were obliged to attend the more, and
did attend, to what was going on, on the stage
—because a word lost would have been a
chasm, which it was impossible for them to
fill up. With such reflections we consoled our
pride then—and I appeal to you, whether, as
a woman, I met generally with less attention
and accommodation, than I have done since
in more expensive situations in the house?
The getting in indeed, and the crowding up
those inconvenient staircases, was bad enough
—but there was still a law of civility to woman
recognised to quite as great an extent as we
ever found in the other passages—and how a
little difficulty overcome heightened the snug
seat, and the play, afterwards! Now we can
only pay our money and walk in. You cannot
see, you say, in the galleries now. I am sure we
saw, and heard too, well enough then—but sight,
and all, I think, is gone with our poverty.

" There was pleasure in eating strawberries,
before they became quite common—in the
first dish of peas, while they were yet dear—
to have them for a nice supper, a treat. What
treat can we have now? If we were to treat
ourselves now—that is, to have dainties a
little above our means, it would be selfish and
wicked. It is very little more than we allow

ourselves beyond what the actual poor can get at, that makes what I call a treat—when two people living together, as we have done, now and then indulge themselves in a cheap luxury, which both like ; while each apologises, and is willing to take both halves of the blame to his single share. I see no harm in people making much of themselves in that sense of the word. It may give them a hint how to make much of others. But now—what I mean by the word—we never do make much of ourselves. None but the poor can do it. I do not mean the veriest poor of all, but persons as we were, just above poverty.

" I know what you are going to say, that it is mighty pleasant at the end of the year to make all meet,—and much ado we used to have every Thirty-first Night of December to account for our exceedings—many a long face did you make over your puzzled accounts, and in contriving to make it out how we had spent so much—or that we had not spent so much—or that it was impossible we should spend so much next year—and still we found our slender capital decreasing—but then, betwixt ways, and projects, and compromises of one sort or another, and talk of curtailing this charge, and doing without that for the future —and the hope that youth brings, and laughing spirits (in which you were never poor till now)

we pocketed up our loss, and in conclusion, with
' lusty brimmers ' (as you used to quote it out
of *hearty cheerful Mr. Cotton,* as you called him),
we used to welcome in the ' coming guest.' Now
we have no reckoning at all at the end of the
old year—no flattering promises about the new
year doing better for us."

Bridget is so sparing of her speech on most
occasions, that when she gets into a rhetorical
vein, I am careful how I interrupt it. I could
not help, however, smiling at the phantom
of wealth which her dear imagination had
conjured up out of a clear income of a poor
—— hundred pounds a year. " It is true we
were happier when we were poorer, but we
were also younger, my cousin. I am afraid
we must put up with the excess, for if we were
to shake the superfluous into the sea, we
should not much mend ourselves. That we
had much to struggle with, as we grew up
together, we have reason to be most thankful.
It strengthened, and knit our compact closer.
We could never have been what we have been
to each other, if we had always had the
sufficiency which you now complain of. The
resisting power—those natural dilations of the
youthful spirit, which circumstances cannot
straiten—with us are long since passed away.
Competence to age is supplementary youth,
a sorry supplement indeed, but I fear the best

that is to be had. We must ride, where we formerly walked : live better, and lie softer —and shall be wise to do so—than we had means to do in those good old days you speak of. Yet could those days return—could you and I once more walk our thirty miles a-day— could Bannister and Mrs. Bland again be young, and you and I be young to see them— could the good old one-shilling gallery days return—they are dreams, my cousin, now— but could you and I at this moment, instead of this quiet argument, by our well-carpeted fireside, sitting on this luxurious sofa—be once more struggling up those inconvenient stair- cases, pushed about, and squeezed, and elbowed by the poorest rabble of poor gallery scramblers—could I once more hear those anxious shrieks of yours—and the delicious *Thank God, we are safe*, which always followed when the topmost stair, conquered, let in the first light of the whole cheerful theatre down beneath us—I know not the fathom line that ever touched a descent so deep as I would be willing to bury more wealth in than Crœsus had, or the great Jew R—— is supposed to have, to purchase it. And now just do look at that merry little Chinese waiter holding an umbrella, big enough for a bed-tester, over the head of that pretty insipid half-Madona-ish chit of a lady in that very blue summer house."

CHARLES LAMB

[1775–1834]

CAPTAIN JACKSON

AMONG the deaths in the obituary for
this month, I observe with concern,
"At his cottage on the Bath Road,
Captain Jackson." The name and the attribu-
tion are common enough ; but a feeling like
reproach persuades me, that this could have
been no other in fact than my dear old friend,
who some five-and-twenty years ago rented a
tenement, which he was pleased to dignify
with the appellation here used, about a mile
from Westbourn Green. Alack, how good men,
and the good turns they do us, slide out of
memory, and are recalled but by the surprise
of some such sad memento as that which now
lies before us !

He whom I mean was a retired half-pay
officer, with a wife and two grown-up daughters,
whom he maintained with the port and notions
of gentlewomen upon that slender professional
allowance. Comely girls they were too.

CHARLES LAMB

And was I in danger of forgetting this man ?
—his cheerful suppers—the noble tone of
hospitality, when first you set your foot in
the cottage—the anxious ministerings about you,
where little or nothing (God knows) was to be
ministered.—Althea's horn in a poor platter—
the power of self-enchantment, by which, in
his magnificent wishes to entertain you, he
multiplied his means to bounties.

You saw with your bodily eyes indeed what
seemed a bare scrag—cold savings from the
foregone meal—remnant hardly sufficient to
send a mendicant from the door contented.
But in the copious will—the revelling imagination of your host—the " mind, the mind,
Master Shallow," whole beeves were spread
before you—hecatombs—no end appeared to
the profusion.

It was the widow's cruse—the loaves and
fishes ; carving could not lessen nor helping
diminish it—the stamina were left—the ele-
mental bone still flourished, divested of its
accidents.

" Let us live while we can," methinks I hear
the open-handed creature exclaim ; " while we
have, let us not want ; " " here is plenty left ; "
" want for nothing "—with many more such
hospitable sayings, the spurs of appetite, and
old concomitants of smoking boards, and feast-
oppressed charges. Then sliding a slender

114

ratio of Single Gloucester upon his wife's plate, or the daughters', he would convey the remnant rind into his own, with a merry quirk of " the nearer the bone," &c., and declaring that he universally preferred the outside. For we had our table distinctions, you are to know, and some of us in a manner sate above the salt. None but the guest or guests dreamed of tasting flesh luxuries at night, the fragments were *verè hospitibus sacra*. But of one thing or another there was always enough, and leavings : only he would sometimes finish the remainder crust, to show that he wished no savings.

Wine we had none; nor, except on very rare occasions, spirits ; but the sensation of wine was there. Some thin kind of ale I remember—" British beverage," he would say. " Push about, my boys ; " " Drink to your sweethearts, girls." At every meagre draught a toast must ensue, or a song. All the forms of good liquor were there, with none of the effects wanting. Shut your eyes, and you could swear a capacious bowl of punch was foaming in the centre, with beams of generous Port or Madeira radiating to it from each of the table corners. You got flustered without knowing whence ; tipsy upon words ; and reeled under the potency of his unperforming Bacchanalian encouragements.

We had our songs—" Why, Soldiers, Why "
—and the " British Grenadiers "—in which last
we were all obliged to bear chorus. Both the
daughters sang. Their proficiency was a
nightly theme—the masters he had given them
—the " no-expense " which he spared to
accomplish them in a science " so necessary
to young women." But then—they could not
sing " without the instrument."

Sacred, and, by me, never-to-be-violated,
Secrets of Poverty ! Should I disclose your
honest aims at grandeur, your makeshift
efforts of magnificence ? Sleep, sleep, with all
thy broken keys, if one of the bunch be extant ;
thrummed by a thousand ancestral thumbs ;
dear, cracked spinnet of dearer Louisa ! Without mention of mine, be dumb, thou thin
accompanier of her thinner warble ! A veil
be spread over the dear delighted face of the
well-deluded father, who now haply listening
to cherubic notes, scarce feels sincerer pleasure
than when she awakened thy time-shaken
chords responsive to the twitterings of that
slender image of a voice.

We were not without our literary talk either.
It did not extend far, but as far as it went, it
was good. It was bottomed well ; had good
grounds to go upon. In *the cottage* was a room,
which tradition authenticated to have been the
same in which Glover, in his occasional

retirements, had penned the greater part of his Leonidas. This circumstance was nightly quoted, though none of the present inmates, that I could discover, appeared ever to have met with the poem in question. But that was no matter. Glover had written there, and the anecdote was pressed into the account of the family importance. It diffused a learned air through the apartment, the little side casement of which (the poet's study window), opening upon a superb view as far as the pretty spire of Harrow, over domains and patrimonial acres, not a rood nor square yard whereof our host could call his own, yet gave occasion to an immoderate expansion of—vanity shall I call it ?—in his bosom, as he showed them in a glowing summer evening. It was all his, he took it all in, and communicated rich portions of it to his guests. It was a part of his largess, his hospitality ; it was going over his grounds ; he was lord for the time of showing them, and you the implicit lookers-on to his magnificence.

He was a juggler, who threw mists before your eyes—you had no time to detect his fallacies. He would say, " Hand me the *silver* sugar tongs " ; and before you could discover that it was a single spoon, and that *plated*, he would disturb and captivate your imagination by a misnomer of " the urn " for a tea kettle ; or by calling a homely bench a

CHARLES LAMB

sofa. Rich men direct you to their furniture, poor ones divert you from it ; he neither did one nor the other, but by simply assuming that everything was handsome about him, you were positively at a demur what you did, or did not see, at *the cottage*. With nothing to live on, he seemed to live on every thing. He had a stock of wealth in his mind ; not that which is promptly termed *Content*, for in truth he was not to be *contained* at all, but over-flowed all bounds by the force of a magnificent self-delusion.

Enthusiasm is catching; and even his wife, a sober native of North Britain, who generally saw things more as they were, was not proof against the continual collision of his credulity. Her daughters were rational and discreet young women ; in the main, perhaps, not insensible to their true circumstances. I have seen them assume a thoughtful air at times. But such was the preponderating opulence of his fancy, that I am persuaded, not for any half hour together did they ever look their own prospects fairly in the face. There was no resisting the vortex of his temperament. His riotous imagination conjured up handsome settlements before their eyes, which kept them up in the eye of the world too, and seem at last to have realised themselves; for they both have married since, I am told, more than respectably.

118

CAPTAIN JACKSON

It is long since, and my memory waxes dim on some subjects, or I should wish to convey some notion of the manner in which the pleasant creature described the circumstances of his own wedding-day. I faintly remember something of a chaise and four, in which he made his entry into Glasgow on that morning to fetch the bride home, or carry her thither, I forget which. It so completely made out the stanza of the old ballad—

> "When we came down through Glasgow town,
> We were a comely sight to see;
> My love was clad in black velvet,
> And I myself in cramasie."

I suppose it was the only occasion, upon which his own actual splendour at all corresponded with the world's notions on that subject. In homely cart, or travelling caravan, by whatever humble vehicle they chanced to be transported in less prosperous days, the ride through Glasgow came back upon his fancy, not as a humiliating contrast, but as a fair occasion for reverting to that one day's state. It seemed an " equipage etern " from which no power of fate or fortune, once mounted, had power thereafter to dislodge him.

There is some merit in putting a handsome face upon indigent circumstances. To bully and swagger away the sense of them before strangers, may not be always discommendable. Tibbs, and Bobadil, even when detected, have more of our admiration than contempt. But for a man to put the cheat upon himself; to play the Bobadil at home; and, steeped in poverty up to the lips, to fancy himself all the while chin-deep in riches, is a strain of constitutional philosophy, and a mastery over fortune, which was reserved for my old friend Captain Jackson.

CHARLES LAMB

[1775–1834]

IMPERFECT SYMPATHIES

I am of a constitution so general, that it consorts and sympathiseth with all things; I have no antipathy, or rather idiosyncracy in anything. Those national repugnances do not touch me, nor do I behold with prejudice the French, Italian, Spaniard, or Dutch,

RELIGIO MEDICI.

THAT the author of the Religio Medici, mounted upon the airy stilts of abstraction, conversant about notional and conjectural essences; in whose categories of Being the possible took the upper hand of the actual; should have overlooked the impertinent individualities of such poor concretions as mankind, is not much to be admired. It is rather to be wondered at, that in the genius of animals he should have condescended to distinguish that species at all. For myself— earth-bound and fettered to the scene of my activities—

"Standing on earth, not rapt above the sky,"

CHARLES LAMB

I confess that I do not feel the differences of mankind, national or individual, to an unhealthy excess. I can look with no indifferent eye upon things or persons. Whatever is, is to me a matter of taste or distaste; or when once it becomes indifferent, it begins to be disrelishing. I am, in plainer words, a bundle of prejudices—made up of likings and dislikings—the veriest thrall to sympathies, apathies, antipathies. In a certain sense, I hope it may be said of me that I am a lover of my species. I can feel for all indifferently, but I cannot feel towards all equally. The more purely-English word that expresses sympathy will better explain my meaning. I can be a friend to a worthy man, who upon another account cannot be my mate or *fellow*. I cannot *like* all people alike.*

I have been trying all my life to like Scotchmen, and am obliged to desist from the experiment in despair. They cannot like me—and in truth, I never knew one of that nation who attempted to do it. There is something more

---

* I would be understood as confining myself to the subject of *imperfect sympathies*. To nations or classes of men there can be no direct *antipathy*. There may be individuals born and constellated so opposite to another individual nature, that the same sphere cannot hold them. I have met with my moral antipodes, and can believe the story of two persons meeting (who never

IMPERFECT SYMPATHIES

plain and ingenuous in their mode of proceeding. We know one another at first sight. There is an order of imperfect intellects (under which mine must be content to rank) which in its constitution is essentially anti-Caledonian. The owners of the sort of faculties I allude to, have minds rather suggestive than comprehensive. They have no pretences to much clearness or precision in their ideas, or in their manner of expressing them. Their intellectual wardrobe (to confess fairly) has few whole pieces in it. They are content with fragments and scattered pieces of Truth. She presents no full front to them—a feature or side-face at

saw one another before in their lives) and instantly fighting.

> " . . . We by proof find there should be
> 'Twixt man and man such an antipathy,
> That though he can show no just reason why
> For any former wrong or injury,
> Can neither find a blemish in his fame,
> Nor aught in face or feature justly blame,
> Can challenge or accuse him of no evil,
> Yet notwithstanding hates him as a devil."

The lines are from old Heywood's " Hierarchie of Angels," and he subjoins a curious story in confirmation, of a Spaniard who attempted to assassinate a King Ferdinand of Spain, and being put to the rack, could give no other reason for the deed but an inveterate antipathy which he had taken to the first sight of the King :

> " . . . The cause which to that act compell'd him
> Was, he ne'er loved him since he first beheld him."

the most. Hints and glimpses, germs and crude essays at a system, is the utmost they pretend to. They beat up a little game per-adventure—and leave it to knottier heads, more robust constitutions, to run it down. The light that lights them is not steady and polar, but mutable and shifting; waxing, and again waning. Their conversation is accordingly. They will throw out a random word in or out of season, and be content to let it pass for what it is worth. They cannot speak always as if they were upon their oath—but must be understood, speaking or writing, with some abatement. They seldom wait to mature a proposition, but e'en bring it to market in the green ear. They delight to impart their defective discoveries as they arise, without waiting for their full development. They are no systematisers, and would but err more by attempting it. Their minds, as I said before, are suggestive merely. The brain of a true Caledonian (if I am not mistaken) is consti-tuted upon quite a different plan. His Minerva is born in panoply. You are never admitted to see his ideas in their growth—if, indeed, they do grow, and are not rather put together upon principles of clockwork. You never catch his mind in an undress. He never hints or suggests any thing, but unlades his stock of ideas in perfect order and completeness. He brings his total wealth into company, and gravely unpacks it. His riches are always about him. He never stoops to catch a glittering something in your presence, to share it with you, before he quite knows whether it be true touch or not. You cannot cry *halves* to any thing that he finds. He does not find but bring. You never witness his first apprehension of a thing. His understanding is always at its meridian—you never see the first dawn, the early streaks. He has no falterings of self-suspicion. Surmises, guesses, misgivings, half-intuitions, semi-consciousness, partial illuminations, dim instincts, embryo conceptions, have no place in his brain, or vocabulary. The twilight of dubiety never falls upon him. Is he orthodox—he has no doubts. Is he an infidel—he has none either. Between the affirmative and the negative there is no borderland with him. You cannot hover with him upon the confines of truth, or wander in the maze of a probable argument. He always keeps the path. You cannot make excursions with him—for he sets you right. His taste never fluctuates. His morality never abates. He cannot compromise, or understand middle actions. There can be but a right and a wrong. His conversation is as a book. His affirmations have the sanctity of an oath. You must speak upon the square

125

with him. He stops a metaphor like a
suspected person in an enemy's country. "A
healthy book!" said one of his countrymen
to me, who had ventured to give that appellation to John Buncle—"did I catch rightly
what you said? I have heard of a man in
health, and of a healthy state of body, but I
do not see how that epithet can be properly
applied to a book." Above all, you must
beware of indirect expressions before a Caledonian. Clap an extinguisher upon your
irony, if you are unhappily blest with a vein
of it. Remember you are upon your oath.
I have a print of a graceful female after
Leonardo da Vinci, which I was showing off
to Mr. * * * *. After he had examined it
minutely, I ventured to ask him how he liked
MY BEAUTY (a foolish name it goes by
among my friends)—when he very gravely
assured me, that "he had considerable respect
for my character and talents" (so he was
pleased to say), "but had not given himself
much thought about the degree of my personal
pretensions." The misconception staggered
me, but did not seem much to disconcert him.
Persons of this nation are particularly fond
of affirming a truth—which nobody doubts.
They do not so properly affirm, as annunciate.
They do indeed appear to have such a love
of truth (as if, like virtue, it were valuable

for itself) that all truth becomes equally
valuable, whether the proposition that contains it be new or old, disputed, or such as is
impossible to become a subject of disputation.
I was present not long since at a party of
North Britons, where a son of Burns was
expected ; and happened to drop a silly
expression (in my South British way), that
I wished it were the father instead of the son
—when four of them started up at once to
inform me, that " that was impossible, because
he was dead." An impracticable wish, it
seems, was more than they could conceive.
Swift has hit off this part of their character,
namely their love of truth, in his biting way,
but with an illiberality that necessarily confine
the passages to the margin.* The tediousness
of these people is certainly provoking. I
wonder if they ever tire one another ! In my
early life I had a passionate fondness for the

* " There are some people who think they sufficiently
acquit themselves and entertain their company, with
relating facts of no consequence, not at all out of the
road of such common incidents as happen every day ;
and this I have observed more frequently among the
Scots than any other nation, who are very careful not
to omit the minutest circumstances of time or place ;
which kind of discourse, if it were not a little relieved by
the uncouth terms and phrases, as well as accent and
gesture peculiar to that country, would be hardly tolerable."—*Hints toward an Essay on Conversation.*

poetry of Burns. I have sometimes foolishly
hoped to ingratiate myself with his countrymen by expressing it. But I have always
found that a true Scot resents your admiration
of his compatriot, even more than he would
your contempt of him. The latter he imputes
to your "imperfect acquaintance with many
of the words which he uses"; and the same
objection makes it a presumption in you to
suppose that you can admire him. Thomson
they seem to have forgotten. Smollett they
have neither forgotten nor forgiven for his
delineation of Rory and his companion, upon
their first introduction to our metropolis.
Speak of Smollett as a great genius, and they
will retort upon you Hume's History compared
with *his* Continuation of it. What if the
historian had continued "Humphrey Clinker"?

I have, in the abstract, no disrespect for
Jews. They are a piece of stubborn antiquity,
compared with which Stonehenge is in its
nonage. They date beyond the pyramids.
But I should not care to be in habits of familiar
intercourse with any of that nation. I confess that I have not the nerves to enter their
synagogues. Old prejudices cling about me.
I cannot shake off the story of Hugh of Lincoln.
Centuries of injury, contempt, and hate, on
the one side—of cloaked revenge, dissimula-
tion, and hate, on the other, between our

and their fathers, must, and ought to affect the blood of the children. I cannot believe it can run clear and kindly yet ; or that a few fine words, such as candour, liberality, the light of the nineteenth century, can close up the breaches of so deadly a disunion. A Hebrew is nowhere congenial to me. He is least distasteful on 'Change—for the mercantile spirit levels all distinctions, as all are beauties in the dark. I boldly confess that I do not relish the approximation of Jew and Christian, which has become so fashionable. The reciprocal endearments have, to me, something hypocritical and unnatural in them. I do not like to see the Church and Synagogue kissing and congeeing in awkward postures of an affected civility. If *they* are converted, why do they not come over to us altogether ? Why keep up a form of separation, when the life of it is fled ? If they can sit with us at table, why do they keck at our cookery ? I do not understand these half convertites. Jews christianising—Christians judaising— puzzle me. I like fish or flesh. A moderate Jew is a more confounding piece of anomaly than a wet Quaker. The spirit of the synagogue is essentially *separative*. B——* would have been more in keeping if he had abided by the faith of his forefathers. There is a

* Braham.

CHARLES LAMB

fine scorn in his face, which nature meant to be
of ——Christians. The Hebrew spirit is strong
in him, in spite of his proselytism. He cannot
conquer the Shibboleth. How it breaks out,
when he sings. "The Children of Israel
passed through the Red Sea!" The auditors,
for the moment, are as Egyptians to him, and
he rides over our necks in triumph. There is
no mistaking him. B—— has a strong expression of sense in his countenance, and it
is confirmed by his singing. The foundation of
his vocal excellence is sense. He sings with
understanding, as Kemble delivered dialogue.
He would sing the Commandments, and give
an appropriate character to each prohibition.
His nation, in general, have not over-sensible
countenances. How should they?—but you
seldom see a silly expression among them.
Gain, and the pursuit of gain, sharpen a man's
visage. I never heard of an idiot being born
among them. Some admire the Jewish female
physiognomy. I admire it—but with trembling. Jael had those full dark inscrutable
eyes.

In the Negro countenance you will often
meet with strong traits of benignity. I have
felt yearnings of tenderness towards some of
these faces—or rather masks—that have
looked out kindly upon one in casual en-
counters in the streets and highways. I love

what Fuller beautifully calls—these "images of God cut in ebony." But I should not like to · associate with them, to share my meals and my good-nights with them—because they are black.

I love Quaker ways, and Quaker worship. I venerate the Quaker principles. It does me good for the rest of the day when I meet any of their people in my path. When I am ruffled or disturbed by any occurrence, the sight, or quiet voice of a Quaker, acts upon me as a ventilator, lightening the air, and taking off a load from the bosom. But I cannot like the Quakers (as Desdemona would say) "to live with them." I am all over sophisticated—with humours, fancies, craving hourly sympathy. I must have books, pictures, theatres, chit-chat, scandal, jokes, ambiguities, and a thousand whim-whams, which their simpler taste can do without. I should starve at their primitive banquet. My appetites are too high for the salads which (according to Evelyn) Eve dressed for the angel, my gusto too excited

To sit a guest with Daniel at his pulse.

The indirect answers which Quakers are often found to return to a question put to them may be explained, I think, without the vulgar assumption, that they are more given to evasion and equivocating than other people.

131

They naturally look to their words more carefully, and are more cautious of committing themselves. They have a peculiar character to keep up on this head. They stand in a manner upon their veracity. A Quaker is by law exempted from taking an oath. The custom of resorting to an oath in extreme cases, sanctified as it is by all religious antiquity, is apt (it must be confessed) to introduce into the laxer sort of minds the notion of two kinds of truth—the one applicable to the solemn affairs of justice, and the other to the common proceedings of daily intercourse. As truth bound upon the conscience by an oath can be but truth, so in the common affirmations of the shop and the market-place a latitude is expected, and conceded upon questions wanting this solemn covenant. Something less than truth satisfies. It is common to hear a person say, " You do not expect me to speak as if I were upon my oath." Hence a great deal of incorrectness and inadvertency, short of falsehood, creeps into ordinary conversation ; and a kind of secondary or laic-truth is tolerated, where clergy-truth—oath-truth, by the nature of the circumstances, is not required. A Quaker knows none of this distinction. His simple affirmation being received, upon the most sacred occasions, without any further test, stamps a value upon the words which he is to use upon the most indifferent topics of life. He looks to them, naturally, with more severity. You can have of him no more than his word. He knows, if he is caught tripping in a casual expression, he forfeits, for himself, at least, his claim to the invidious exemption. He knows that his syllables are weighed—and how far a consciousness of this particular watchfulness, exerted against a person, has a tendency to produce indirect answers, and a diverting of the question by honest means might be illustrated, and the practice justified, by a more sacred example than is proper to be adduced upon this occasion. The admirable presence of mind, which is notorious in Quakers upon all contingencies, might be traced to this imposed self-watchfulness—if it did not seem rather an humble and secular scion of that old stock of religious constancy, which never bent or faltered in the Primitive Friends, or gave way to the winds of persecution, to the violence of judge or accuser, under trials and racking examinations. " You will never be the wiser, if I sit here answering your questions till midnight," said one of those upright Justices to Penn, who had been putting law-cases with a puzzzling subtlty. " Thereafter as the answers may be," retorted the Quaker. The astonishing composure of

CHARLES LAMB

this people is sometimes ludicrously displayed
in lighter instances. I was travelling in a
stage coach with three male Quakers, buttoned
up in the straitest non-conformity of their
sect. We stopped to bait at Andover, where
a meal, partly tea apparatus, partly supper,
was set before us. My friends confined themselves to the tea-table. I in my way took
supper. When the landlady brought in the
bill, the eldest of my companions discovered
that she had charged for both meals. This
was resisted. Mine hostess was very clamorous
and positive. Some mild arguments were used
on the part of the Quakers, for which the
heated mind of the good lady seemed by no
means a fit recipient. The guard came in
with his usual peremptory notice. The
Quakers pulled out their money, and formally
tendered it—so much for tea—I, in humble
imitation, tendering mine—for the supper
which I had taken. She would not relax in
her demand. So they all three quietly put up
their silver, as did myself, and marched out
of the room, the eldest and gravest going first,
with myself closing up the rear, who thought
I could not do better than follow the example
of such grave and warrantable personages.
We got in. The steps went up. The coach
drove off. The murmurs of mine hostess, not
very indistinctly or ambiguously pronounced,

became after a time inaudible—and now my conscience, which the whimsical scene had for a time suspended, beginning to give some twitches, I waited, in the hope that some justification would be offered by these serious persons for the seeming injustice of their conduct. To my great surprise, not a syllable was dropped on the subject. They sat as mute as at a meeting. At length the eldest of them broke silence, by inquiring of his next neighbour, "Hast thee heard how indigos go at the India House?" and the question operated as a soporific on my moral feeling as far as Exeter.

WILLIAM HAZLITT

[1778–1830]

MERRY ENGLAND

" St. George for merry England ! "

THIS old-fashioned epithet might be supposed to have been bestowed ironically, or on the old principle— *Ut lucus a non lucendo.* Yet there is something in the sound that hits the fancy, and a sort of truth beyond appearances. To be sure, it is from a dull, homely ground that the gleams of mirth and jollity break out, but the streaks of light that tinge the evening sky are not the less striking on that account. The beams of the morning sun shining on the lonely glades, or through the idle branches of the tangled forest, the leisure, the freedom, " the pleasure of going and coming without knowing where," the troops of wild deer, the sports of the chase, and other rustic gambols, were sufficient to justify the well-known appellation of " Merry Sherwood," and in like manner, we may apply the phrase to *Merry*

MERRY ENGLAND

England. The smile is not the less sincere
because it does not always play upon the
cheek ; and the jest is not the less welcome,
nor the laugh less hearty, because they
happen to be a relief from care or leaden-eyed
melancholy. The instances are the more
precious as they are rare ; and we look forward to them with the greater good-will, or
back upon them with the greater gratitude, as
we drain the last drop in the cup with particular
relish. If not always gay or in good spirits,
we are glad when any occasion draws us out
of our natural gloom, and disposed to make
the most of it. We may say with *Silence* in
the play, " I have been merry once ere now "
—and this once was to serve him all his life ;
for he was a person of wonderful silence and
gravity, though " he chirped over his cups,"
and announced with characteristic glee that
" there were pippins and cheese to come."
Silence was in this sense a merry man, that is,
he would be merry if he could, and a very
great economy of wit, like very slender fare,
was a banquet to him, from the simplicity of
his taste and habits. " Continents," says
Hobbs, " have most of what they contain—
and in this view it may be contended that
the English are the merriest people in the
world, since they only show it on high-days
and holidays. They are then like a school-boy

WILLIAM HAZLITT

let loose from school, or like a dog that has slipped his collar. They are not gay like the French, who are one eternal smile of self-complacency, tortured into affectation, or spun out into languid indifference, nor are they voluptuous and immersed in sensual indolence, like the Italians ; but they have that sort of intermittent, fitful, irregular gaiety, which is neither worn out by habit, nor deadened by passion, but is sought with avidity as it takes the mind by surprise, is startled by a sense of oddity and incongruity, indulges its wayward humours or lively impulses, with perfect freedom and lightness of heart, and seizes occasion by the forelock, that it may return to serious business with more cheerfulness, and have something to beguile the hours of thought or sadness. I do not see how there can be high spirits without low ones ; and everything has its price according to circumstances. Perhaps we have to pay a heavier tax on pleasure, than some others : what skills it, so long as our good spirits and good hearts enable us to bear it ?

" They " (the English), says Froissart, " amused themselves sadly after the fashion of their country "—*ils se rejouissoient tristement selon la coutume de leur pays.* They have indeed a way of their own. Their mirth is a

138

relaxation from gravity, a challenge to dull care to be gone ; and one is not always clear at first, whether the appeal is successful. The cloud may still hang on the brow ; the ice may not thaw at once. To help them out in their new character is an act of charity. Anything short of hanging or drowning is something to begin with. They do not enter into their amusements the less doggedly because they may plague others. They like a thing the better for hitting them a rap on the knuckles, for making their blood tingle. They do not dance or sing, but they make good cheer —" eat, drink, and are merry." No people are fonder of field-sports, Christmas gambols, or practical jests. Blindman's-buff, hunt-the-slipper, hot-cockles, and snap-dragon, are all approved English games, full of laughable surprises and " hair-breadth 'scapes," and serve to amuse the winter fireside after the roast-beef and plum-pudding, the spiced ale and roasted crab, thrown (hissing-hot) into the foaming tankard. Punch (not the liquor, but the puppet) is not, I fear, of English origin ; but there is no place, I take it, where he finds himself more at home or meets a more joyous welcome, where he collects greater crowds at the corners of streets, where he opens the eyes or distends the cheeks wider, or where the bangs and blows, the uncouth gestures, ridiculous anger, and screaming voice of the chief performer excite more boundless merriment or louder bursts of laughter among all ranks and sorts of people. An English theatre is the very throne of pantomine; nor do I believe that the gallery and boxes of Drury Lane or Covent Garden filled on the proper occasion with holiday folks (big or little) yield the palm for undisguised, tumultuous, inextinguishable laughter to any spot in Europe. I do not speak of the refinement of the mirth (this is no fastidious speculation) but of its cordiality, on the return of these long-looked-for and licensed periods; and I may add here, by way of illustration, that the English common people are a sort of grown children, spoiled and sulky perhaps, but full of glee and merriment, when their attention is drawn off by some sudden and striking object. The May-pole is almost gone out of fashion among us; but May-day, besides its flowering hawthorns and its pearly dews, has still its boasted exhibition of painted chimney-sweepers and their Jack-o-the-green, whose tawdry finery, bedizened faces, unwonted gestures, and short-lived pleasures call forth good-humoured smiles and looks of sympathy in the spectators. There is no place where trap-ball, fives, prison-base, football, quoits, bowls are better understood or

more successfully practised; and the very
names of a cricket bat and ball make English
fingers tingle. What happy days must " Long
Robinson " have passed in getting ready his
wickets and mending his bats, who, when two
of the fingers of his right hand were struck
off by the violence of a ball, had a screw
fastened to it to hold the bat, and with the
other hand still sent the ball thundering
against the boards that bounded *Old Lord's
cricket-ground*! What delightful hours must
have been his in looking forward to the
matches that were to come, in recounting the
feats he had performed in those that were
past! I have myself whiled away whole
mornings in seeing him strike the ball (like
a countryman mowing with a scythe) to the
farthest extremity of the smooth, level, sun-
burnt ground; and with long, awkward
strides count the notches that made victory
sure! Then again, cudgel-playing, quarter-
staff, bull and badger-baiting, cock-fighting
are almost the peculiar diversions of this
island, and often objected to us as barbarous
and cruel; horse-racing is the delight and
ruin of numbers; and the noble science of
boxing is all our own. Foreigners can scarcely
understand how we can squeeze pleasure out
of this pastime; the luxury of hard blows
given or received; the joy of the ring; the

141

perseverance of the combatants.*   The English

* " The gentle and free passage of arms at Ashby " was, we are told, so called by the chroniclers of the time, on account of the feats of horsemanship and the quantity of knightly blood that was shed.   This last circumstance was perhaps necessary to qualify it with the epithet of " gentle," in the opinion of some of these historians.   I think the reason why the English are the bravest nation on earth is, that the thought of blood or a delight in cruelty is not the chief excitement with them.   Where it is, there is necessarily a *reaction* ; for though it may add to our eagerness and savage ferocity in inflicting wounds, it does not enable us to endure them with greater patience. The English are led to the attack or sustain it equally well, because they fight as they box, not out of malice, but to show *pluck* and manhood. *Fair play and old England for ever !* This is the only bravery that will stand the test.   There is the same determination and spirit shown in resistance as in attack ; but not the same pleasure in getting a cut with a sabre as in giving one.   There is, therefore, always a certain degree of effeminacy mixed up with any approach to cruelty, since both have their source in the same principle, viz., an overvaluing of pain.[1]   This was the reason the French (having the best cause and the best general in the world) ran away at Waterloo, because they were inflamed, furious, drunk with the blood of their enemies, but when it came to their turn, wanting the same stimulus, they were panic-struck, and their hearts and their senses failed them all at once.

[1] Vanity is the same half-witted principle, compared with pride.   It leaves men in the lurch when it is most needed ; is mortified at being reduced to stand on the defensive, and relinquishes the field to its more surly antagonist.

also excel, or are not excelled in wiring a hare, in stalking a deer, in shooting, fishing, and hunting. England to this day boasts her Robin Hood and his merry men, that stout archer and outlaw and patron-saint of the sporting calendar. What a cheerful sound is that of the hunters, issuing from the autumnal wood and sweeping over hill and dale!

> " . . . A cry more tuneable
> Was never halloo'd to by hound or horn."

What sparkling richness in the scarlet coats of the riders, what a glittering confusion in the pack, what spirit in the horses, what eagerness in the followers on foot, as they disperse over the plain, or force their way over hedge and ditch! Surely, the coloured prints and pictures of these, hung up in gentlemen's halls and village alehouses, however humble, as works of art, have more life and health and spirit in them, and mark the pith and nerve of the national character more creditably than the mawkish, sentimental, affected designs of Theseus and Pirithous, and Æneas and Dido, pasted on foreign *salons à manger*, and the interior of country-houses. If our tastes are not epic, nor our pretensions lofty, they are simple and our own; and we may possibly enjoy our native rural sports and the rude remembrances of them, with the truer relish on this account, that they are suited to us and we to them. The English nation, too, are naturally " brothers of the angle." This pursuit implies just that mixture of patience and pastime, of vacancy and thoughtfulness, of idleness and business, of pleasure and of pain, which is suited to the genius of an Englishman, and as I suspect, of no one else in the same degree. He is eminently gifted to stand in the situation assigned by Dr. Johnson to the angler, " at one end of a rod with a worm at the other." I should suppose no other language than ours can show such a book as an often-mentioned one, Walton's *Complete Angler*—so full of *naïveté*, of un-affected sprightliness, of busy trifling, of dainty songs, of refreshing brooks, of shady arbours, of happy thoughts and of the herb called *Heart's Ease*! Some persons can see neither the wit nor wisdom of this genuine volume, as if a book as well as a man might not have a personal character belonging to it, amiable, venerable from the spirit of joy and thorough goodness it manifests, independently of acute remarks or scientific discoveries ; others object to the cruelty of Walton's theory and practice of trout-fishing—for my part I should as soon charge an infant with cruelty for killing a fly, and I feel the same sort of pleasure in reading his book as I should

have done in the company of this happy,
childlike old man, watching his ruddy cheek,
his laughing eye, the kindness of his heart, and
the dexterity of his hand in seizing his finny
prey ! It must be confessed there is often an
odd sort of *materiality* in English sports and
recreations. I have known several persons,
whose existence consisted wholly in manual
exercises, and all whose enjoyments lay at
their finger-ends. Their greatest happiness
lay in cutting a stick, in mending a cabbage-
net, in digging a hole in the ground, in hitting
a mark, turning a lathe, or in something else
of the same kind, at which they had a certain
knack. Well is it when we can amuse ourselves with such trifles and without injury to
others ! This class of character, which the
Spectator has immortalised in the person of
Will Wimble, is still common among younger
brothers and retired gentlemen of small
incomes in town or country. London is half
suburbs. The suburbs of Paris are a desert,
and you see nothing but crazy windmills,
stone walls, and a few straggling visitants, in
spots where in England you would find a
thousand villas, a thousand terraces, crowned
with their own delights, or be stunned with
the noise of bowling-greens and tea-gardens,
or stifled with the fumes of tobacco mingling
with fragrant shrubs, or the clouds of dust

K   145

raised by half the population of the metropolis panting and toiling in search of a mouthful of fresh air. The Parisian is, perhaps, as well (or better) contented with himself wherever he is, stewed in his shop or his garret; the Londoner is miserable in these circumstances, and glad to escape from them.* Let no one object to the gloomy appearance of a London Sunday, compared with a Parisian one. It is a part of our politics and our religion: we would not have James the First's *Book of Sports* thrust down our throats: and besides, it is part of our character to do one thing at a time, and not to be dancing a jig and on our knees in the same breath. It is true the Englishman spends his Sunday evening at the ale-house—

> "And e'en on Sunday
> He drinks with Kirton Jean till Monday . . ."

but he only unbends and waxes mellow by degrees, and sits soaking till he can neither sit, stand, nor go: it is his vice, and a beastly one it is, but not a proof of any inherent distaste to mirth or good fellowship. Neither can foreigners throw the carnival in our teeth with any effect: those who have seen it (at Florence, for example), will say that it

* The English are fond of change of scene; the French of change of posture; the Italians like to sit still, and do nothing.

146

MERRY ENGLAND

is duller than anything in England. Our Bartholomew Fair is Queen Mab herself to it ! What can be duller than a parcel of masks moving about the streets and looking as grave and monotonous as possible from day to day, and with the same lifeless formality in their limbs and gestures as in their features ? One might as well expect variety and spirit in a procession of wax-work figures. We must be hard run indeed, when we have recourse to a pasteboard proxy to set off our mirth: a mask may be a very good cover for licentious-ness (though of that I saw no signs), but it is a very bad exponent of wit and humour. I should suppose there is more drollery and unction in the caricatures in Fore's shop-window, than in all the masks in Italy, without exception.*

The humour of English writing and description has often been wondered at ; and it flows

* Bells are peculiar to England. They jangle them in Italy during the carnival as boys do with us at Shrove-tide ; but they have no notion of ringing them. The sound of village bells never cheers you in travelling, nor have you the lute or cittern in their stead. The expression of " Merry Bells " is a favourite, and not one of the least appropriate in our language :

" For him the merry bells had rung, I ween,
If in this nook of quiet bells had ever been."
Castle of Indolence.[1]

[1] Canto i, st. 62.

from the same source as the merry *traits* of our character. A degree of barbarism and rusticity seems necessary to the perfection of humour. The droll and laughable depend on peculiarity and incongruity of character. But with the progress of refinement, the peculiarities of individuals and of classes wear out or lose their sharp, abrupt edges ; nay, a certain slowness and dulness of understanding is required to be struck with odd and unaccountable appearances, for which a greater facility of apprehension can sooner assign an explanation that breaks the force of the seeming absurdity, and to which a wider scope of imagination is more easily reconciled. Clowns and country people are more amused, are more disposed to laugh and make sport of the dress of strangers, because from their ignorance the surprise is greater, and they cannot conceive anything to be natural or proper to which they are unused. Without a given portion of hardness and repulsiveness of feeling the ludicrous cannot well exist. Wonder and curiosity, the attributes of inexperience, enter greatly into its composition. Now it appears to me that the English are (or were) just at that mean point between intelligence and obtuseness, which must produce the most abundant and happiest crop of humour. Absurdity and singularity glide over the

MERRY ENGLAND

French mind without jarring or jostling with it ; or they evaporate in levity : with the Italians they are lost in indolence or pleasure. The ludicrous takes hold of the English imagination, and clings to it with all its ramifications. We resent any difference or peculiarity of appearance at first, and yet, having not much malice at our hearts, we are glad to turn it into a jest—we are liable to be offended, and as willing to be pleased—struck with oddity from not knowing what to make of it, we wonder and burst out a laughing at the eccentricity of others, while we follow our own bent from wilfulness or simplicity, and thus afford them, in our turn, matter for the indulgence of the comic vein. It is possible that a greater refinement of manners may give birth to finer distinctions of satire and a nicer tact for the ridiculous : but our insular situation and character are, I should say, most likely to foster, as they have in fact fostered, the greatest quantity of natural and striking humour, in spite of our plodding tenaciousness, and want both of gaiety and quickness of perception. A set of raw recruits with their awkward movements and unbending joints are laughable enough : but they cease to be so, when they have once been drilled into discipline and uniformity. So it is with nations that lose their angular points and grotesque qualities with education and intercourse : but it is in a mixed state of manners that comic humour chiefly flourishes, for, in order that the drollery may not be lost, we must have spectators of the passing scene who are able to appreciate and embody its most remarkable features—wits as well as *butts* for ridicule. I shall mention two names in this department which may serve to redeem the national character from absolute dulness and solemn pretence—Fielding and Hogarth. These were thorough specimens of true English humour ; yet both were grave men. In reality, too high a pitch of animal spirits runs away with the imagination, instead of helping it to reach the goal ; is inclined to take the jest for granted when it ought to work it out with patient and marked touches, and it ends in vapid flippancy and impertinence. Among our neighbours on the Continent, Molière and Rabelais carried the freedom of wit and humour to an almost incredible height ; but they rather belonged to the old French school, and even approach and exceed the English licence and extravagance of conception. I do not consider Congreve's wit (though he belongs to us) as coming under the article here spoken of ; for his genius is anything but *merry*. Lord Byron was in the habit of railing at the spirit of our good old comedy, and of abusing Shake-

MERRY ENGLAND

speare's Clowns and Fools, which he said the
refinement of the French and Italian stage
would not endure, and which only our gross-
ness and puerile taste could tolerate. In this
I agree with him ; and it is *pat* to my purpose.
I flatter myself that we are almost the only
people who understand and relish *nonsense*.
We are not " merry and wise," but indulge
our mirth to excess and folly. When we trifle,
we trifle in good earnest ; and having once
relaxed our hold of the helm, drift idly down
the stream, and, delighted with the change,
are tossed about " by every little breath " of
whim or caprice,

> " That under Heaven is blown."

All we then want is to proclaim a truce with
reason, and to be pleased with as little expense
of thought or pretension to wisdom as possible.
This licensed fooling is carried to its very
utmost length in Shakespeare, and in some
other of our elder dramatists, without, perhaps,
sufficient warrant or the same excuse. Nothing
can justify this extreme relaxation but extreme
tension. Shakespeare's trifling does indeed
tread upon the very borders of vacancy : his
meaning often hangs by the very slenderest
threads. For this he might be blamed if he
did not take away our breath to follow his
eagle flights, or if he did not at other times

151

WILLIAM HAZLITT

make the cordage of our hearts crack. After our heads ache with thinking, it is fair to play the fool. The clowns were as proper an appendage to the gravity of our antique literature, as fools and dwarfs were to the stately dignity of courts and noble houses in former days. Of all people, they have the best right to claim a total exemption from rules and rigid formality, who, when they have anything of importance to do, set about it with the greatest earnestness and persever-ance, and are generally grave and sober to a proverb.* Swift, who wrote more idle or *nonsense* verses than any man, was the severest of moralists ; and his feelings and observations morbidly acute. Did not Lord Byron himself follow up his *Childe Harold* with his *Don Juan* ?—not that I insist on what he did as an illustration of the English character. He was one of the English Nobility, not one of the English people ; and his occasional ease and familiarity were in my mind equally con-strained and affected, whether in relation to the pretensions of his rank or the efforts of his genius.

They ask you in France, how you pass your time in England without amusements ; and

* The strict formality of French serious writing is resorted to as a foil to the natural levity of their character.

can with difficulty believe that there are theatres in London, still less that they are larger and handsomer than those in Paris. That we should have comic actors, " they own surprises them." They judge of the English character in the lump as one great jolter-head, containing all the stupidity of the country, as the large ball at the top of the Dispensary in Warwick Lane, from its resemblance to a gilded pill, has been made to represent the whole pharmacopœia and professional quackery of the kingdom. They have no more notion, for instance, how we should have such an actor as Liston on our stage, than if we were to tell them we have parts performed by a sea-otter; nor, if they were to see him, would they be much the wiser, or know what to think of his unaccountable twitches of countenance or nondescript gestures, or his teeth chattering in his head, his eyes that seem dropping from their sockets, his nose that is tickled by a jest as by a feather, and shining with self-complacency as if oiled, his ignorant conceit, his gaping stupor, his lumpish vivacity in Lubin Log or Tony Lumpkin; for as our rivals do not wind up the machine to such a determined intensity of purpose, neither have they any idea of its running down to such degrees of imbecility and folly, or coming to an absolute *stand-still*

and lack of meaning, nor can they enter into
or be amused with the contrast. No people
ever laugh heartily who can give a reason for
doing so : and I believe the English in general
are not yet in this predicament. They are not
metaphysical, but very much in a state of
nature ; and this is one main ground why
I give them credit for being merry, notwithstanding appearances. Their mirth is not the
mirth of vice or desperation, but of innocence
and a native wildness. They do not cavil or
boggle at niceties, or merely come to the edge
of a joke, but break their necks over it with
a wanton " Here goes," where others make a
pirouette and stand upon decorum. The
French cannot, however, be persuaded of the
excellence of our comic stage, nor of the store
we set by it. When they ask what amusements we have, it is plain they can never have
heard of Mrs. Jordan, nor King, nor Bannister,
not Suett, nor Munden, nor Lewis, nor little
Simmons, nor Dodd, and Parsons, and Emery,
and Miss Pope, and Miss Farren, and all those
who even in my time have gladdened a
nation and " made life's business like a
summer's dream." Can I think of them, and
of their names that glittered in the play-bills
when I was young, exciting all the flutter of
hope and expectation of seeing them in their
favourite parts of Nell, of Little Pickle, or

Touchstone, or Sir Peter Teazle, or Lenitive
in the *Prize*, or Lingo, or Crabtree, or Nipper-
kin, or old Dornton, or Ranger, or the Copper
Captain, or Lord Sands, or Fitch, or Moses, or
Sir Andrew Aguecheek, or Acres, or Elbow, or
Hodge, or Flora, or the Duenna, or Lady
Teazle, or Lady Grace, or of the gaiety that
sparkled in all eyes, and the delight that over-
flowed all hearts, as they glanced before us in
these parts,

> "Throwing a gaudy shadow upon life,"

and not feel my heart yearn within me, or
couple the thoughts of England and the spleen
together ? Our cloud has at least its rainbow
tints ; ours is not one long polar night of cold
and dulness, but we have the gleaming lights
of fancy to amuse us, the household fires of
truth and genius to warm us. We can go to a
play and see Liston ; or stay at home and
read *Roderick Random ;* or have Hogarth's
prints of *Marriage à la Mode* hanging round
our room. Tut ! " there's livers " even in
England, as well as " out of it." We are not
quite the *forlorn hope* of humanity, the last
of nations. The French look at us across the
Channel, and seeing nothing but water and a
cloudy mist, think that this is England. If
they have any farther idea of us, it is of
George III and our Jack tars, the House of

Lords and House of Commons ; and this is no great addition to us. To go beyond this, to talk of arts and elegances as having taken up their abode here, or to say that Mrs. Abington was equal to Mademoiselle Mars, and that we at one time got up the *School for Scandal*, as they do the *Misanthrope*, is to persuade them that Iceland is a pleasant winter retreat, or to recommend the whale-fishery as a classical amusement. The French are the *cockneys* of Europe, and have no idea how any one can exist out of Paris, or be alive without incessant grimace and *jabber*. Yet what imports it ? What ! Though the joyous train I have just enumerated were, perhaps, never heard of in the precincts of the Palais-Royal, is it not enough that they gave pleasure where they were, to those who saw and heard them ? Must our laugh, to be sincere, have its echo on the other side of the water ? Had not the French their favourites and their enjoyments at the time, that we knew nothing of ? Why then should we not have ours (and boast of them too) without their leave ? A monopoly of self-conceit is not a monopoly of all other advantages. The English, when they go abroad, do not take away the prejudice against them by their looks. We seem duller and sadder than we are. As I write this, I am sitting in the open

air in a beautiful valley, near Vevy : Clarens
is on my left, the Dent de Jamant is behind
me, the rocks of Meillerie opposite : under my
feet is a green bank, enamelled with white and
purple flowers, in which a dewdrop here and
there still glitters with pearly light—

> " And gaudy butterflies flutter round."

Intent upon the scene and upon the thoughts
that stir within me, I conjure up the cheerful
passages of my life, and a crowd of happy
images appear before me. No one would see
it in my looks—my eyes grow dull and fixed,
and I seem rooted to the spot, as all this
phantasmagoria passes in review before me,
glancing a reflex lustre on the face of the world
and nature. But the traces of pleasure, in
my case, sink into an absorbent ground of
thoughtful melancholy, and require to be
brought out by time and circumstances, or
(as the critics tell you) by the *varnish* of
style !

The *comfort*, on which the English lay so
much stress, is of the same character, and
arises from the same source as their mirth.
Both exist by contrast and a sort of contradic-
tion. The English are certainly the most uncomfortable of all people in themselves, and
therefore it is that they stand in need of every
kind of comfort and accommodation. The

least thing puts them out of their way, and therefore everything must be in its place. They are mightily offended at disagreeable tastes and smells, and therefore they exact the utmost neatness and nicety. They are sensible of heat and cold, and therefore they cannot exist, unless everything is snug and warm, or else open and airy, where they are. They must have "all applicances and means to boot." They are afraid of interruption and intrusion, and therefore they shut themselves up in indoor enjoyments and by their own firesides. It is not that they require luxuries (for that implies a high degree of epicurean indulgence and gratification), but they cannot do without *their comforts ;* that is, whatever tends to supply their physical wants, and ward off physical pain and annoyance. As they have not a fund of animal spirits and enjoyments in themselves, they cling to external objects for support, and derive solid satisfaction from the ideas of order, cleanliness, plenty, property, and domestic quiet, as they seek for diversion from odd accidents and grotesque surprises, and have the highest possible relish not of voluptuous softness, but of hard knocks and dry blows, as one means of ascertaining their personal identity.

WILLIAM HAZLITT

[1778–1830]

THE FIGHT

" . . . *The* fight, *the* fight's *the thing,*
Wherein I'll catch the conscience of the king."

*W*HERE *there's a will, there's a way.*—
I said so to myself, as I walked
down Chancery Lane, about half-
past six o'clock on Monday the 10th of
December, to inquire at Jack Randall's where
the fight the next day was to be ; and I found
the proverb nothing " musty " in the present
instance. I was determined to see this fight,
come what would, and see it I did in great
style. It was my *first fight,* yet it more
than answered my expectations. . . .

I was going down Chancery Lane, thinking
to ask at Jack Randall's where the fight was
to be, when, looking through the glass-door
of the Hole in the Wall, 1 heard a gentleman
asking the same question *at* Mrs. Randall, as the
author of " Waverley " would express it. Now
Mrs. Randall stood answering the gentleman's

question, with all the authenticity of the Lady of the Champion of the Light Weights. Thinks I, I'll wait till this person comes out, and learn from him how it is. For, to say a truth, I was not fond of going into this house-of-call for heroes and philosophers, ever since the owner of it (for Jack is no gentleman) threatened once upon a time to kick me out of doors for wanting a mutton-chop at his hospitable board, when the conqueror in thirteen battles was more full of *blue rain* than of good manners. I was the more mortified at this repulse, inasmuch as I heard Mr. James Simpkins, hosier in the Strand, one day when the character of the Hole in the Wall was brought in question, observe, "The house is a very good house, and the company quite genteel: I have been there myself!" Remembering this unkind treatment of mine host, to which mine hostess was also a party, and not wishing to put her in unquiet thoughts at a time jubilant like the present, I waited at the door, when who should issue forth but my friend Joe P——s, and seeing him turn suddenly up Chancery Lane with that quick jerk and impatient stride which distinguish a lover of the FANCY, I said, "I'll be hanged if that fellow is not going to the fight, and is on his way to get me to go with him." So it proved in effect, and we

agreed to adjourn to my lodgings to discuss
measures with that cordiality which makes old
friends like new, and new friends like old, on
great occasions. We are cold to others only
when we are dull in ourselves, and have neither
thoughts nor feelings to impart to them. Give
a man a topic in his head, a throb of pleasure in
his heart, and he will be glad to share it with
the first person he meets. Joe and I, though
we seldom meet, were an *alter idem* on this
memorable occasion, and had not an idea that
we did not candidly impart ; and " so carelessly did we fleet the time," that I wish no
better, when there is another fight, than to
have him for a companion, on my journey
down, and to return with my friend Jack
Pigott, talking of what was to happen or of
what did happen, with a noble subject always
at hand, and liberty to digress to others whatever they offered. Indeed, on my repeating
the lines from Spencer in an involuntary fit of
enthusiasm,

> " What more felicity can fall to creature,
> Than to enjoy delight with liberty ? "

my last-named ingenious friend stopped me
by saying that this, translated into the vulgate,
meant " *Going to see a fight.*"

Joe and I could not settle about the method
of going down. He said there was a caravan,

he understood, to start from Tom Belcher's at two, which would go there *right out* and back again the next day. Now, I never travel all night, and said I should get a cast to Newbury by one of the mails. Joe swore the thing was impossible, and I could only answer that I had made up my mind to it. In short, he seemed to me to waver, said he only came to see if I was going, had letters to write, a cause coming on the day after, and faintly said at parting (for I was bent on setting out that moment), " Well, we meet at Philippi ? " I made the best of my way to Piccadilly. The mail-coach stand was bare. " They are all gone," said I ; " this is always the way with me—in the instant I lose the future—if I had not stayed to pour out that last cup of tea, I should have been just in time ; "—and cursing my folly and ill-luck together, without inquiring at the coach-office whether the mails were gone or not, I walked on in despite, and to punish my own dilatoriness and want of determination. At any rate, I would not turn back ; I might get to Hounslow, or perhaps farther, to be on my road the next morning. I passed Hyde Park Corner (my Rubicon), and trusted to fortune. Suddenly I heard the clattering of a Brentford stage, and the fight rushed full upon my fancy. I argued (not unwisely) that even a Brentford coachman

was better company than my own thoughts
(such as they were just then), and at his
invitation mounted the box with him. I
immediately stated my case to him—namely,
my quarrel with myself for missing the Bath
or Bristol mail, and my determination to get
on in consequence as well.as I could, without
any disparagement or insulting comparison
between longer or shorter stages. It is a
maxim with me that stage-coaches, and consequently stage-coachmen, are respectable in
proportion to the distance they have to travel ;
so I said nothing on that subject to my Brentford friend. Any incipient tendency to an
abstract proposition, or (as he might have
construed it) to a personal reflection of this
kind, was, however, nipped in the bud ; for
I had no sooner declared indignantly that I
had missed the mails, that he flatly denied
that they were gone along, and lo ! at the
instant three of them drove by in rapid, provoking, orderly succession, as if they would
devour the ground before them. Here again
I seemed in the contradictory situation of the
man in Dryden who exclaims,

"I follow Fate, which does too hard pursue ! "

If I had stopped to inquire at the White
Horse Cellar, which would not have taken me
a minute, I should now have been driving

WILLIAM HAZLITT

down the road in all the dignified unconcern and *ideal* perfection of mechanical conveyance. The Bath mail I had set my mind upon, and I had missed it, as I miss everything else, by my own absurdity, in putting the will for the deed, and aiming at ends without employing means. " Sir," said he of the Brentford, " the Bath mail will be up presently ; my brother-in-law drives it, and I will engage to stop him if there is a place empty." I almost doubted my good genius ; but, sure enough, up it drove like lightning, and stopped directly at the call of the Brentford Jehu. I would not have believed this possible, but the brother-in-law of a mail-coach driver is himself no mean man. I was transferred without loss of time from the top of one coach to that of the other, desired the guard to pay my fare to the Brentford coachman for me, as I had no change, was accommodated with a greatcoat, put up my umbrella to keep off a drizzling mist, and we began to cut through the air like an arrow. The milestones disappeared one after another, the rain kept off ; Tom Turtle* the trainer sat before me on the coach-box, with whom I exchanged civilities as a gentleman going to the fight : the passion that had transported me an hour before was subdued to pensive regret and conjectural musing on the next

* John Thurtell, to wit.

164

day's battle; I was promised a place inside at Reading, and upon the whole I thought myself a lucky fellow. Such is the force of imagination! On the outside of any other coach on the 10th of December, with a Scotch mist drizzling through the cloudy moonlight air, I should have been cold, comfortless, impatient, and, no doubt, wet through; but seated on the Royal-mail, I felt warm and comfortable; the air did me good, the ride did me good, I was pleased with the progress we had made, and confident that all would go well through the journey. When I got inside at Reading, I found Turtle and a stout valetudinarian, whose costume bespoke him one of the FANCY, and who had risen from a three months' sick-bed to get into the mail to see the fight. They were intimate, and we fell into a lively discourse. My friend the trainer was confined in his topics to fighting dogs and men, to bears and badgers; beyond this he was " quite chapfallen," not a word to throw at a dog, or indeed very wisely fell asleep, when any other game was started. The whole art of training (I, however, learnt from him) consists in two things, exercise and abstinence, abstinence and exercise, repeated alternately and without end. A yolk of an egg with a spoonful of rum in it is the first thing in a morning, and then a walk of six miles till breakfast. This meal consists of a plentiful supply of tea and toast and beefsteaks. Then another six or seven miles till dinner-time. and another supply of solid beef or mutton with a pint of porter, and perhaps, at the utmost, a couple of glasses of sherry. Martin trains on water, but this increases his infirmity on another very dangerous side. The Gas-man takes now and then a chirping glass (under the rose) to console him, during a six weeks' probation, for the absence of Mrs. Hickman— an agreeable woman, with (I understand) a pretty fortune of two hundred pounds. How matter presses on me! What stubborn things are facts! How inexhaustible is nature and art! " It is well," as I once heard Mr. Richmond observe, " to see a variety." He was speaking of cock-fighting as an edifying spectacle. I cannot deny but that one learns more of what *is* (I do not say of what *ought to be*) in this desultory mode of practical study than from reading the same book twice over, even though it should be a moral treatise. Where was I ? I was sitting at dinner with the candidate for the honours of the ring, " where good digestion waits on appetite, and health on both." Then follows an hour of social chat and native glee ; and afterwards, to another breathing over heathy hill or dale.

THE FIGHT

Back to supper, and then to bed, and up by six again—our hero

"Follows so the ever-running sun,
With profitable *ardour* . . . "

to the day that brings him victory or defeat in the green fairy circle. Is not this life more sweet than mine ? I was going to say ; but I will not libel any life by comparing it to mine, which is (at the date of these presents) bitter as coloquintida, and the dregs of aconitum !

The invalid in the Bath mail soared a pitch above the trainer, and did not sleep so sound, because he had "more figures and more fantasies." We talked the hours away merrily. He had faith in surgery, for he had three ribs set right, that had been broken in a *turn-up* at Belcher's, but thought physicians old women, for they had no antidote in their catalogue for brandy. An indigestion is an excellent commonplace for two people that never met before. By way of ingratiating myself, I told him the story of my doctor, who, on my earnestly representing to him that I thought his regimen had done me harm, assured me that the whole pharmacopœia contained nothing comparable to the prescription he had given me ; and, as a proof of its undoubted efficacy, said that " he had had one gentleman with my complaint under his hands for the last fifteen years."

167

WILLIAM HAZLITT

This anecdote made my companion shake
the rough sides of his three greatcoats with
boisterous laughter ; and Turtle, starting out
of his sleep, swore he knew how the fight would
go, for he had had a dream about it. Sure
enough, the rascal told us how the three first
rounds went off, but " his dream," like others,
" denoted a foregone conclusion." He knew
his men. The moon now rose in silver state,
and I ventured, with some hesitation, to point
out this object of placid beauty, with the blue
serene beyond, to the man of science, to which
his ear he " seriously inclined," the more as
it gave promise *d'un beau jour*, and showed
the ring undrenched by envious showers,
arrayed in sunny smiles. Just then, all going
on well, I thought on my friend Joe, whom I
had left behind, and said innocently, " There
was a blockhead of a fellow I left in town,
who said there was no possibility of getting
down by the mail, and talked of going by a
caravan from Belcher's at two in the morning,
after he had written some letters." " Why,"
said he of the lapels, " I should not wonder if
that was the very person we saw running about
like mad from one coach-door to another, and
asking if anyone had seen a friend of his, a
gentleman going to the fight, whom he had
missed stupidly enough by staying to write
a note." " Pray, sir," said my fellow-

traveller, " had he a plaid-cloak on ? " " Why
no," said I, " not at the time I left him, but
he very well might afterwards, for he offered
to lend me one." The plaid-cloak and the
letter decided the thing. Joe, sure enough,
was in the Bristol mail, which preceded us by
about fifty yards. This was droll enough.
We had now but a few miles to our place of
destination, and the first thing I did on alight-
ing at Newbury, both coaches stopping at the
same time, was to call out, " Pray, is there a
gentleman in that mail of the name of
P——s ? " " No," said Joe, borrowing something of the vein of Gilpin, " for I have just
got out." " Well," says he, " this is lucky ;
but you don't know how vexed I was to miss
you ; for," added he, lowering his voice, " do
you know when I left you I went to Belcher's
to ask about the caravan, and Mrs. Belcher
said, very obligingly, she couldn't tell about
that, but there were two gentlemen had taken
places by the mail and were gone on in a
landau, and she could frank us. It's a pity
I didn't meet with you ; we could then have
got down for nothing. But *mum's the word*."
It's the devil for anyone to tell me a secret,
for it is sure to come out in print. I do not
care so much to gratify a friend, but the
public ear is too great a temptation to me.

Our present business was to get beds and

supper at an inn ; but this was no easy task. The public-houses were full, and where you saw a light at a private house, and people poking their heads out of the casement to see what was going on, they instantly put them in and shut the window, the moment you seemed advancing with a suspicious overture for accommodation. Our guard and coachman thundered away at the outer gate of the Crown for some time without effect—such was the greater noise within ; and when the doors were unbarred and we got admittance, we found a party assembled in the kitchen round a good hospitable fire, some sleeping, others drinking, talking on politics and on the fight. A tall English yeoman (something like Matthews in the face, and quite as great a wag)—

"A lusty man to ben an abbot able,"

was making such a prodigious noise about rent and taxes, and the price of corn now and formerly, that he had prevented us from being heard at the gate. The first thing I heard him say was to a shuffling fellow who wanted to be off a bet for a shilling glass of brandy and water : "Confound it, man, don't be *insipid !*" Thinks I, that is a good phrase. It was a good omen. He kept it up so all night, nor flinched with the approach of morning. He was a fine fellow, with sense, wit, and spirit, a hearty body and a joyous mind, free-spoken, frank, convivial—one of that true English breed that went with Harry the Fifth to the siege of Harfleur—" standing like greyhounds in the slips," etc. We ordered tea and eggs (beds were soon found to be out of the question), and this fellow's conversation was *sauce piquante*. It did one's heart good to see him brandish his oaken towel and to hear him talk. He made mincemeat of a drunken, stupid, red-faced, quarrelsome, frowsy farmer, whose nose " he moralised into a thousand similes," making it out a firebrand like Bardolph's. " I'll tell you what, my friend," says he, " the landlady has only to keep you here to save fire and candle. If one was to touch your nose, it would go off like a piece of charcoal." At this the other only grinned like an idiot, the sole variety in his purple face being his little peering grey eyes and yellow teeth ; called for another glass, swore he would not stand it ; and after many attempts to provoke his humorous antagonist to single combat, which the other turned off (after working him up to a ludicrous pitch of choler) with great adroitness, he fell quietly asleep with a glass of liquor in his hand, which he could not lift to his head. His laughing persecutor made a speech over him, and turning to the opposite side of the room,

WILLIAM HAZLITT

where they were all sleeping in the midst of
this " loud and furious fun," said, " There's a
scene, by G–d ! for Hogarth to paint. I think
he and Shakespeare were our two best men at
copying life." This confirmed me in my
good opinion of him. Hogarth, Shakespeare,
and Nature were just enough for him, (indeed
for any man) to know. I said, " You read
Cobbett, don't you ? At least," says I,
" you talk just as well as he writes." He
seemed to doubt this. But I said, " We have
an hour to spare ; if you'll get pen, ink, and
paper, and keep on talking, I'll write down
what you say ; and if it doesn't make a capital
' Political Register,' I'll forfeit my head. You
have kept me alive to-night, however. I
don't know what I should have done without
you." He did not dislike this view of the
thing, nor my asking if he was not about the
size of Jem Belcher ; and told me soon afterwards, in the confidence of friendship, that
the circumstance which had given him nearly
the greatest concern in his life was Cribb's
beating Jem after he had lost his eye by racket-
playing. The morning dawns; that dim but
yet clear light appears, which weighs like
solid bars of metal on the sleepless eyelids ;
the guests dropped down from their chambers
one by one—but it was too late to think of
going to bed now (the clock was on the stroke

172

THE FIGHT

of seven) ; we had nothing for it but to find
a barber's (the pole that glittered in the
morning sun lighted us to his shop), and then
a nine miles march to Hungerford. The day
was fine, the sky was blue, the mists retiring
from the marshy ground, the path was tolerably dry, the sitting-up all night had not done
us much harm—at least the cause was good ;
we talked of this and that with amicable
difference, roving and sipping of many subjects, but still invariably we returned to the
fight. At length, a mile to the left of Hungerford, on a gentle eminence, we saw the ring,
surrounded by covered carts, gigs, and carriages, of which hundreds had passed us on
the road; Joe gave a youthful shout, and we
hastened down a narrow lane to the scene
of action.

Reader, have you ever seen a fight ? If
not, you have a pleasure to come, at least if
it is a fight like that between the Gas-man and
Bill Neate. The crowd was very great when
we arrived on the spot ; open carriages were
coming up, with streamers flying and music
playing, and the country people were pouring
in over hedge and ditch in all directions, to see
their hero beat or be beaten. The odds were
still on Gas, but only about five to four.
Gully had been down to try Neate, and had
backed him considerably, which was a damper

to the sanguine confidence of the adverse party. About £200,000 was pending. Gas says he has lost £3,000, which were promised him by different gentlemen if he had won. He had presumed too much on himself, which had made others presume on him. This spirited and formidable young fellow seems to have taken for his motto the old maxim, that "there are three things necessary to success in life—*Impudence! Impudence! Impudence!*" It is so in matters of opinion, but not in the FANCY, which is the most practical of all things, though even here confidence is half the battle, but only half. Our friend had vapoured and swaggered too much, as if he wanted to grin and bully his adversary out of the fight. "Alas! the Bristol man was not so tamed!" "This is the *grave-digger*" (would Tom Hickman exclaim in the moments of intoxication from gin and success, showing his tremendous right hand) ; "this will send many of them to their long homes ; I haven't done with them yet!" Why should he—though he had licked four of the best men within the hour—why should he threaten to inflict dishonourable chastisement on my old master Richmond, a veteran going off the stage, and who has borne his sable honours meekly? Magnanimity, my dear Tom, and bravery should be inseparable. Or why should he go up to his antagonist, the first time he ever saw him at the Fives-court, and measuring him from head to foot with a glance of contempt, as Achilles surveyed Hector, say to him, " What, are you Bill Neate ? I'll knock more blood out of that great carcase of thine, this day fortnight, than you ever knocked out of a bullock's ! " It was not manly, 'twas not fighter-like. If he was sure of the victory (as he was not) the less said about it the better. Modesty should accompany the FANCY as its shadow. The best men were always the best behaved. Jem Belcher, the Game Chicken (before whom the Gas-man could not have lived), were civil, silent men. So is Cribb ; so is Tom Belcher, the most elegant of sparrers, and not a man for every one to take by the nose. I enlarged on this topic in the mail (while Turtle was asleep), and said very wisely (as I thought) that impertinence was a part of no profession. A boxer was bound to beat his man, but not to thrust his fist, either actually or by implication, in every one's face. Even a highwayman, in the way of trade, may blow out your brains, but if he uses foul language at the same time, I should say he was no gentleman. A boxer, I would infer, need not be a blackguard or a coxcomb, more than another.

175

Perhaps I press this point too much on a fallen man—Mr. Thomas Hickman has by this time learnt that first of all lessons, " That man was made to mourn." He has lost nothing by the late fight but his presumption ; and that every man may do as well without. By an over display of this quality, however, the public had been prejudiced against him, and the *knowing ones* were taken in. Few but those who had bet on him wished Gas to win. With my own prepossessions on the subject, the result of the 11th of December appeared to me as fine a piece of poetical justice as I had ever witnessed. The difference of weight between the two combatants (fourteen stone to twelve) was nothing to the sporting men. Great, heavy, clumsy, long-armed Bill Neate kicked the beam in the scale of the Gas-man's vanity. The amateurs were frightened at his big words, and thought they would make up for the difference of six feet and five-feet nine. Truly, the FANCY are not men of imagination. They judge of what has been, and cannot conceive of anything that is to be. The Gas-man had won hitherto ; therefore he must beat a man half as big again as himself— and that to a certainty. Besides, there are as many feuds, factions, prejudices, pedantic notions, in the FANCY as in the State or in the schools. Mr. Gully is almost the only

THE FIGHT

cool, sensible man among them, who exercises
an unbiassed discretion, and is not a slave to
his passions in these matters. But enough of
reflections, and to our tale. The day, as I
have said, was fine for a December morning.
The grass was wet and the ground miry, and
ploughed up with multitudinous feet, except
that, within the ring itself, there was a spot of
virgin-green, closed in and unprofaned by
vulgar tread, that shone with dazzling brightness in the midday sun. For it was now noon,
and we had an hour to wait. This is the
trying time. It is then the heart sickens, as
you think what the two champions are about,
and how short a time will determine their
fate. After the first blow is struck there is
no opportunity for nervous apprehensions ;
you are swallowed up in the immediate
interest of the scene—but

> " Between the acting of a dreadful thing
> And the first motion, all the interim is
> Like a phantasm, or a hideous dream."

I found it so as I felt the sun's rays clinging
to my back, and saw the white wintry clouds
sink below the verge of the horizon. " So,"
I thought, " my fairest hopes have faded from
my sight !—so will the Gas-man's glory, or
that of his adversary, vanish in an hour."
The *swells* were parading in their white

boxcoats, the outer ring was cleared with some
bruises on the heads and shins of the rustic
assembly (for the *Cockneys* had been distanced
by the sixty-six miles ; the time drew near ;
I had got a good stand ; a bustle, a buzz, ran
through the crowd ; and from the opposite
side entered Neate, between his second and
bottle-holder. He rolled along, swathed in
his loose greatcoat, his knock-knees bending
under his huge bulk ; and, with a modest
cheerful air, threw his hat into the ring. He
then just looked round, and begun quietly to
undress ; when from the other side there was
a similar rush and an opening made, and the
Gas-man came forward with a conscious air
of anticipated triumph, too much like the
cock-of-the-walk. He strutted about more
than became a hero, sucked oranges with a
supercilious air, and threw away the skin
with a toss of his head, and went up and
looked at Neate, which was an act of supererogation. The only sensible thing he did was,
as he strode away from the modern Ajax, to
fling out his arms, as if he wanted to try
whether they would do their work that day.
By this time they had stripped, and presented
a strong contrast in appearance. If Neate
was like Ajax, " with Atlantean shoulders,
fit to bear " the pugilistic reputation of all
Bristol, Hickman might be compared to

THE FIGHT

Diomed, light, vigorous, elastic, and his back
glistened in the sun, as he moved about, like
a panther's hide. There was now a dead
pause—attention was awestruck. Who, at
that moment, big with a great event, did not
draw his breath short—did not feel his heart
throb? All was ready. They tossed up for
the sun, and the Gas-man won. They were
led up to the *scratch*—shook hands, and went
at it.

In the first round every one thought it was
all over. After making play a short time, the
Gas-man flew at his adversary like a tiger,
struck five blows in as many seconds, three
first, and then following him as he staggered
back, two more, right and left, and down he
fell, a mighty ruin. There was a shout, and I
said, " There is no standing this." Neate
seemed like a lifeless lump of flesh and bone,
round which the Gas-man's blows played with
the rapidity of electricity or lightning, and
you imagined he would only he lifted up to be
knocked down again. It was as if Hickman
held a sword or a fire in that right hand of his,
and directed it against an unarmed body.
They met again, and Neate seemed, not cowed,
but particularly cautious. I saw his teeth
clenched together and his brows knit close
against the sun. He held out both his arms
at full length straight before him, like two

179

sledge-hammers, and raised his left an inch or two higher. The Gas-man could not get over this guard—they struck mutually and fell, but without advantage on either side. It was the same in the next round ; but the balance of power was thus restored—the fate of the battle was suspended. No one could tell how it would end. This was the only moment in which opinion was divided ; for, in the next, the Gas-man, aiming a mortal blow at his adversary's neck with his right hand, and failing from the length he had to reach, the other returned it with his left at full swing, planted a tremendous blow on his cheek-bone and eyebrow, and made a red ruin of that side of his face. The Gas-man went down, and there was another shout—a roar of triumph as the waves of fortune rolled tumultuously from side to side. This was a settler. Hickman got up, and " grinned horrible a ghastly smile," yet he was evidently dashed in his opinion of himself ; it was the first time he had ever been so punished ; all one side of his face was perfect scarlet, and his right eye was closed in dingy blackness, as he advanced to the fight, less confident, but still determined. After one or two rounds, not receiving another such remembrance, he rallied and went at it with his former impetuosity. But in vain. His strength had been weakened—his blows could not tell at such a distance—he was obliged to fling himself at his adversary, and could not strike from his feet; and almost as regularly as he flew at him with his right hand, Neate warded the blow, or drew back out of its reach, and felled him with the return of his left. There was little cautious sparring—no half-hits—no tapping and trifling, none of the *petit-maitreship* of the art—they were almost all knock-down blows : the fight was a good stand-up fight. The wonder was the half-minute time. If there had been a minute or more allowed between each round, it would have been intelligible how they should by degrees recover strength and resolution ; but to see two men smashed to the ground, smeared with gore, stunned, senseless, the breath beaten out of their bodies ; and then, before you recover from the shock, to see them rise up with new strength and courage, stand ready to inflict or receive mortal offence, and rush upon each other " like two clouds over the Caspian "—this is the most astonishing thing of all : this is the high and heroic state of man ! From this time forward the event became more certain every round ; and about the twelfth it seemed as if it must have been over. Hickman generally stood with his back to me ; but in the scuffle he had changed positions, and Neate then made a tremendous lunge at him, and hit him full in the face. It was doubtful whether he would fall backwards or forwards; he hung suspended for a minute or two, and then fell back, throwing his hands in the air, and with his face lifted up to the sky. I never saw anything more terrific than his aspect just before he fell. All traces of life, of natural expression, were gone from him. His face was like a human skull, a death's-head spouting blood. The eyes were filled with blood, the nose streamed with blood, the mouth gaped blood. He was not like an actual man, but like a preternatural, spectral appearance, or like one of the figures in Dante's "Inferno." Yet he fought on after this for several rounds, still striking the first desperate blow, and Neate standing on the defensive, and using the same cautious guard to the last, as if he had still all his work to do; and it was not till the Gas-man was so stunned in the seventeenth or eighteenth round that his senses forsook him, and he could not come to time, that the battle was declared over. Ye who despise the FANCY, do something to show as much pluck or as much self-possession as this, before you assume a superiority which you have never given a single proof of by any one action in the whole course of your lives! When the Gas-man came to himself, the first words he uttered were, " Where am I ? What

is the matter ? " "Nothing is the matter,
Tom, you have lost the battle, but you are the
bravest man alive." And Jackson whispered
to him, " I am collecting a purse for you,
Tom." Vain sounds, and unheard at that
moment ! Neate instantly went up and shook
him cordially by the hand, and seeing some
old acquaintance, began to flourish with his
fists, calling out, " Ah ! you always said I
couldn't fight—what do you think now ? "
But all in good-humour, and without any
appearance of arrogance ; only it was evident
Bill Neate was pleased that he had won the
fight. When it was over I asked Cribb if he
did not think it was a good one. He said,
" *Pretty well!* " The carrier-pigeons now
mounted into the air, and one of them flew
with the news of her husband's victory to the
bosom of Mrs. Neate. Alas for Mrs. Hickman !

Mais au revoir, as Sir Fopling Flutter says.
I went down with Joe P——s ; I returned with
Jack Pigott, whom I met on the ground.
Tom's is a rattle-brain ; Pigott is a sentimentalist. Now, under favour, I am a
sentimentalist too—therefore I say nothing,
but that the interest of the excursion did not
flag as I came back. Pigott and I marched
along the causeway leading from Hungerford
to Newbury, now observing the effect of
a brilliant sun on the tawny meads or

moss-coloured cottages, now exulting in the
fight, now digressing to some topic of general
and elegant literature.   My friend was dressed
in character for the occasion, or like one of the
FANCY; that is, with a double portion of
greatcoats, clogs, and overhauls; and just as
we had agreed with a couple of country-lads
to carry his superfluous wearing-apparel to
the next town, we were overtaken by a return
post-chaise, into which I got, Pigott preferring
a seat on the bar.   There were two strangers
already in the chaise, and on their observing
they supposed I had been to the fight, I said
I had, and concluded they had done the same.
They appeared, however, a little shy and sore
on the subject ; and it was not till after several
hints dropped and questions put, that it
turned out that they had missed it.   One of
these friends had undertaken to drive the
other there in his gig : they had set out, to
make sure work, the day before at three in
the afternoon.   The owner of the one-horse
vehicle scorned to ask his way, and drove
right on to Bagshot, instead of turning off at
Hounslow : there they stopped all night, and
set off the next day across the country to
Reading, from whence they took coach, and got
down to within a mile or two of Hungerford,
just half-an-hour after the fight was over.
This might be safely set down as one of the

miseries of human life. We parted with these
two gentlemen who had been to see the fight,
but had returned as they went, at Wolhampton,
where we were promised beds (an irresistible
temptation, for Pigott had passed the preceding
night at Hungerford as we had done at Newbury), and we turned into an old bow-windowed
parlour with a carpet and a snug fire ; and
after devouring a quantity of tea, toast, and
eggs, sat down to consider, during an hour of
philosophic leisure, what we should have for
supper. In the midst of an Epicurean delibera-
tion between a roasted fowl and mutton-chops
with mashed potatoes, we were interrupted by
an inroad of Goths and Vandals—*O procul este
profani*—not real flash-men, but interlopers,
noisy pretenders, butchers from Tothill-fields,
brokers from Whitechapel, who called immediately for pipes and tobacco, hoping it would
not be disagreeable to the gentlemen, and
began to insist that it was *a cross*. Pigott
withdrew from the smoke and noise into
another room, and left me to dispute the
point with them for a couple of hours *sans
intermission* by the dial. The next morning
we rose refreshed ; and on observing that
Jack had a pocket volume in his hand, in
which he read in the intervals of our discourse,
I inquired what it was, and learned, to my
particular satisfaction, that it was a volume

185

of the " New Eloise." Ladies, after this, will
you contend that a love for the FANCY is
incompatible with the cultivation of sentiment ? We jogged on as before, my friend
setting me up in a genteel drab greatcoat and
green silk handkerchief (which I must say
became me exceedingly), and after stretching
our legs for a few miles, and seeing Jack
Randall, Ned Turner, and Scroggins pass on
the top of one of the Bath coaches, we engaged
with the driver of the second to take us to
London for the usual fee. I got inside, and
found three other passengers. One of them
was an old gentleman with an aquiline nose,
powdered hair, and a pigtail, and who looked
as if he had played many a rubber at the Bath
rooms. I said to myself, " He is very like
Mr. Windham ; I wish he would enter into
conversation, that I might hear what fine
observations would come from those finely-
turned features." However, nothing passed,
till, stopping to dine at Reading, some inquiry
was made by the company about the fight,
and I gave (as the reader may believe) an
eloquent and animated description of it.
When we got into the coach again, the old
gentleman, after a graceful exordium, said he
had, when a boy, been to a fight between the
famous Broughton and George Stevenson,
who was called the *Fighting Coachman*, in the

year 1770, with the late Mr. Windham. This beginning flattered the spirit of prophecy within me, and riveted my attention. He went on—" George Stevenson was coachman to a friend of my father's. He was an old man when I saw him some years afterwards. He took hold of his own arm and said, ' There was muscle here once, but now it is no more than this young gentleman's.' He added, ' Well, no matter; I have been here long; I am willing to go hence, and I hope I have done no more harm than another man.' Once," said my unknown companion, " I asked him if he had ever beat Broughton. He said Yes ; that he had fought with him three times, and the last time he fairly beat him, though the world did not allow it. ' I'll tell you how it was, master. When the seconds lifted us up in the last round, we were so exhausted that neither of us could stand, and we fell upon one another, and as Master Broughton fell uppermost, the mob gave it in his favour, and he was said to have won the battle. But the fact was, that as his second (John Cuthbert) lifted him up, he said to him, ' I'll fight no more, I've had enough '; which, says Stevenson, ' you know, gave me the victory. And to prove to you that this was the case, when John Cuthbert was on his deathbed, and they asked him if there was anything on his mind which he wished to confess, he answered, " Yes ; that there was one thing he wished to set right, for that certainly Master Stevenson won the last fight with Master Broughton ; for he whispered him as he lifted him up in the last round of all, that he had had enough." ' This," said the Bath gentleman, " was a bit of human nature "; and I have written this account of the fight on purpose that it might not be lost to the world. He also stated as a proof of the candour of mind in this class of men, that Stevenson acknowledged that Broughton could have beat him in his best day ; but that he (Broughton) was getting old in their last encounter. When we stopped in Piccadilly, I wanted to ask the gentleman some questions about the late Mr. Windham, but had not courage. I got out, resigned my coat and green silk handkerchief to Pigott (loth to part with these ornaments of life), and walked home in high spirits.

P.S.—Joe called upon me the next day to ask me if I did not think the fight was a complete thing. I said I thought it was. I hope he will relish my account of it.

LEIGH HUNT

[1784–1859]

GETTING UP ON COLD MORNINGS

AN Italian author—Giulio Cordara, a Jesuit—has written a poem upon insects, which he begins by insisting that those troublesome and abominable little animals were created for our annoyance, and that they were certainly not inhabitants of Paradise. We of the North may dispute this piece of theology; but, on the other hand, it is as clear as the snow on the house-tops, that Adam was not under the necessity of shaving; and that when Eve walked out of her delicious bower, she did not step upon ice three inches thick.

Some people say it is a very easy thing to get up of a cold morning. You have only, they tell you, to take the resolution, and the thing is done. This may be very true; just as a boy at school has only to take a flogging, and the thing is over. But we have not at all made up our minds upon it; and we find

it a very pleasant exercise to discuss the
matter candidly before we get up. This at
least is not idling, though it may be lying.
It affords an excellent answer to those who
ask how lying in bed can be indulged in by
a reasoning being,—a rational creature. How ?
Why, with the argument calmly at work in
one's head, and the clothes over one's shoulder.
Oh, it is a fine way of spending a sensible,
impartial half-hour.

If these people would be more charitable,
they would get on with their argument better.
But they are apt to reason so ill, and to assert
so dogmatically, that one could wish to have
them stand round one's bed of a bitter
morning, and lie before their faces. They
ought to hear both sides of the bed, the inside
and out. If they cannot entertain themselves
with their own thoughts for half an hour or so,
it is not the fault of those who can. If their
will is never pulled aside by the enticing arms
of imagination, so much the luckier for the
stage-coachman.

Candid inquirers into one's decumbency,
besides the greater or less privileges to be
allowed a man in proportion to his ability of
keeping early hours, the work given his
faculties, &c., will at least concede their due
merits to such representations as the following.
In the first place (says the injured but calm

appealer), I have been warm all night, and find my system in a state perfectly suitable to a warm-blooded animal. To get out of this state into the cold, besides the inharmonious and uncritical abruptness of the transition, in so unnatural to such a creature that the poets, refining upon the tortures of the damned, make one of their greatest agonies consist in being suddenly transported from heat to cold,—from fire to ice. They are " haled " out of their " beds," says Milton, by " harpy-footed furies,"—fellows who come to call them. On my first movement towards the anticipation of getting up, I find that such parts of the sheets and bolster as are exposed to the air of the room are stone-cold. On opening my eyes, the first thing that meets them is my own breath rolling forth, as if in the open air, like smoke out of a cottage chimney. Think of this symptom. Then I turn my eyes sideways, and see the window all frozen over. Think of that. Then the servant comes in. " It is very cold this morning, is it not ? " " Very cold, sir." " Very cold indeed, isn't it ? " " Very cold indeed, sir." " More than usually so, isn't it, even for this weather ? " (Here the servant's wit and good-nature are put to a considerable test, and the inquirer lies on thorns for the answer.) " Why, sir,—I think it *is*." (Good creature! There is not a better or more truth-telling servant going.) " I must rise, however ; get me some warm water." Here comes a fine interval between the departure of the servant and the arrival of the hot water ; during which, of course, it is of " no use " to get up. The hot water comes. " Is it quite hot ? " " Yes, sir." " Perhaps too hot for shaving ; I must wait a little ? " " No, sir ; it will just do." (There is an overnice propriety sometimes, an officious zeal of virtue, a little troublesome.) " Oh, the shirt —you must air my clean shirt ; linen gets very damp this weather." " Yes, sir." Here another delicious five minutes. A knock at the door. " Oh, the shirt—very well. My stockings—I think the stockings had better be aired too." " Very well, sir." Here another interval. At length everything is ready except myself. I now (continues our incumbent—a happy word, by the bye, for a country vicar)—I now cannot help thinking a good deal—who can ?—upon the unnecessary and villainous custom of shaving : it is a thing so unmanly (here I nestle closer)—so effeminate (here I recoil from an unlucky step into the colder part of the bed). No wonder that the Queen of France took part with the rebels against that degenerate king, her husband, who first affronted her smooth

visage with a face like her own. The Emperor
Julian never showed the luxuriancy of his
genius to better advantage than in reviving
the flowing beard. Look at Cardinal Bembo's
picture—at Michael Angelo's—at Titian's—at
Shakspeare's—at Fletcher's—at Spenser's—
at Chaucer's—at Alfred's—at Plato's. I could
name a great man for every tick of my watch.
Look at the Turks, a grave and otiose people.
Think of Haroun al Raschid, and bed-ridden
Hassan. Think of Wortley Montague, the
worthy son of his mother, a man above the
prejudice of his time. Look at the Persian
gentlemen, whom one is ashamed of meeting
about the suburbs, their dress and appearance
are so much finer than our own. Lastly,
think of the razor itself—how totally opposed
to every sensation of bed—how cold, how
edgy, how hard ! how utterly different from
anything like the warm and circling amplitude,
which

> " Sweetly recommends itself
> Unto our gentle senses ! "

Add to this, benumbed fingers, which may help
you to cut yourself, a quivering body, a frozen
towel, and an ewer full of ice ; and he that
says there is nothing to oppose in all this, only
shows, at any rate, that he has no merit in
opposing it.

N   **193**

LEIGH HUNT

Thomson, the poet, who exclaims in his
" Seasons "—

" Falsely luxurious ! Will not man awake ! "

used to lie in bed till noon, because he said
he had no motive in getting up. He could
imagine the good of rising ; but then he could
also imagine the good of lying still ; and his
exclamation, it must be allowed, was made
upon summer-time, not winter. We must
proportion the argument to the individual
character. A money-getter may be drawn
out of his bed by three and fourpence ; but
this will not suffice for a student. A proud
man may say, " What shall I think of myself
if I don't get up ? " but the more humble one
will be content to waive this prodigious notion
of himself, out of respect to his kindly bed.
The mechanical man shall get up without
any ado at all ; and so shall the barometer.
An ingenious lier in bed will find hard matter
of discussion even on the score of health and
longevity. He will ask us for our proofs and
precedents of the ill effects of lying later in
cold weather ; and sophisticate much on the
advantages of an even temperature of body ;
of the natural propensity (pretty universal)
to have one's way ; and of the animals that
roll themselves up, and sleep all the winter.
As to longevity, he will ask whether the longest

life is of necessity the best; and whether
Holborn is the handsomest street in London.

We only know of one confounding, not to
say confounded argument, fit to overturn the
huge luxury, the "enormous bliss," of the
vice in question. A lier in bed may be allowed
to profess a disinterested indifference for his
health or longevity; but while he is showing
the reasonableness of consulting his own, or
one person's comfort, he must admit the
proportionate claim of more than one; and the
best way to deal with him is this, especially
for a lady; for we earnestly recommend the
use of that sex on such occasions, if not somewhat *over*-persuasive; since extremes have an
awkward knack of meeting. First then, admit
all the ingeniousness of what he says, telling
him that the bar has been deprived of an
excellent lawyer. Then look at him in the
most good-natured manner in the world, with
a mixture of assent and appeal in your
countenance, and tell him that you are waiting
breakfast for him; that you never like to
breakfast without him; that you really want
it too; that the servants want theirs; that
you shall not know how to get the house into
order, unless he rises; and that you are sure
he would do things twenty times worse even
than getting out of his warm bed, to put them
all into good humour and a state of comfort.

Then, after having said this, throw in the comparatively indifferent matter, to *him*, about his health ; but tell him that it is no indifferent matter to you ; that the sight of his illness makes more people suffer than one ; but that if, nevertheless, he really does feel so very sleepy and so very much refreshed by——— Yet stay ; we hardly know whether the fraility of a——— Yes, yes ; say that too, especially if you say it with sincerity ; for if the weakness of human nature on the one hand, and the *vis inertiæ* on the other, should lead him to take advantage of it once or twice, good-humour and sincerity form an irresistible junction at last ; and are still better and warmer things than pillows and blankets.

Other little helps of appeal may be thrown in, as occasion requires. You may tell a lover for instance, that lying in bed makes people corpulent ; a father, that you wish him to complete the fine manly example he sets his children ; a lady, that she will injure her bloom or her shape, which M. or W. admires so much ; and a student or artist, that he is always so glad to have done a good day's work in his best manner.

Reader. And pray, Mr. Indicator, how do *you* behave yourself in this respect.

Indicator. Oh, madam, perfectly, of course ; like all advisers.

GETTING UP ON COLD MORNINGS

Reader. Nay, I allow that your mode of argument does not look quite so suspicious as the old way of sermonising and severity, but I have my doubts, especially from that laugh of yours. If I should look in to-morrow morning——

Indicator. Ah, madam, the look in of a face like yours does anything with me. It shall fetch me up at nine, if you please—*six*, I meant to say.

LEIGH HUNT

[1784–1859]

THE OLD GENTLEMAN

OUR Old Gentleman, in order to be exclusively himself, must be either a widower or a bachelor. Suppose the former. We do not mention his precise age, which would be invidious ; nor whether he wears his own hair or a wig, which would be wanting in universality. If a wig, it is a compromise between the more modern scratch and the departed glory of the toupee. If his own hair, it is white, in spite of his favourite grandson, who used to get on the chair behind him, and pull the silver hairs out, ten years ago. If he is bald at top, the hair-dresser, hovering and breathing about him like a second youth, takes care to give the bald place as much powder as the covered ; in order that he may convey to the sensorium within a pleasing indistinctness of idea respecting the exact limits of skin and hair. He is very clean and neat ; and in warm weather is proud of opening his waistcoat half way down, and letting so much of his frill be seen, in order to show his hardiness as well as taste. His watch and shirt-buttons are of the best; and he does not care if he has two rings on a finger. If his watch ever failed him at the club or coffee-house, he would take a walk every day to the nearest clock of good character, purely to keep it right. He has a cane at home, but seldom uses it, on finding it out of fashion with his elderly juniors. He has a small cocked hat for gala days, which he lifts higher from his head than the round one, when made a bow to. In his pockets are two handkerchiefs (one for the neck at night-time), his spectacles, and his pocket-book. The pocket-book, among other things, contains a receipt for a cough, and some verses cut out of an odd sheet of an old magazine, on the lovely Duchess of A., beginning—

"When beauteous Mira walks the plain."

He intends this for a commonplace book which he keeps, consisting of passages in verse and prose cut out of newspapers and magazines, and pasted in columns; some of them rather gay. His principal other books are Shakespeare's plays and Milton's " Paradise Lost "; the *Spectator*; the " History of England "; the works of Lady M. W. Montague, Pope, and Churchill; Middleton's "Geography"; the *Gentleman's Magazine*; Sir John Sinclair on Longevity; several plays with portraits in character; "Account of Elizabeth Canning"; "Memoirs of George Ann Bellamy"; "Poetical Amusements at Bath-Enston"; Blair's works; "Elegant Extracts"; "Junius," as originally published; a few pamphlets on the American War and Lord George Gordon, &c.; and one on the French Revolution. In his sitting-rooms are some engravings from Hogarth and Sir Joshua; an engraved portrait of the Marquis of Granby; ditto of M. le Comte de Grasse surrendering to Admiral Rodney; a humorous piece after Penny; and a portrait of himself, painted by Sir Joshua. His wife's portrait is in his chamber, looking upon his bed. She is a little girl, stepping forward with a smile and a pointed toe, as if going to dance. He lost her when she was sixty.

The Old Gentleman is an early riser, because he intends to live at least twenty years longer. He continues to take tea for breakfast, in spite of what is said against its nervous effects; having been satisfied on that point some years ago by Dr. Johnson's criticism on Hanway, and a great liking for tea previously. His china cups and saucers have been broken

since his wife's death, all but. one, which is
religiously kept for his use. He passes his
morning in walking or riding, looking in at
auctions, looking after his India bonds, or
some such money securities, furthering some
subscription set on foot by his excellent friend
Sir John, or cheapening a new old print for
his portfolio. He also hears of the newspapers ; not caring to see them till after
dinner at the coffee-house. He may also
cheapen a fish or so ; the fishmonger soliciting
his doubting eye as he passes, with a profound
bow of recognition. He eats a pear before dinner.

His dinner at the coffee-house is served up
to him at the accustomed hour, in the old
accustomed way, and by the accustomed
waiter. If William did not bring it, the fish
would be sure to be stale, and the flesh new.
He eats no tart ; or, if he ventures on a little,
takes cheese with it. You might as soon
attempt to persuade him out of his senses, as
that cheese is not good for digestion. He
takes port ; and if he has drunk more than
usual, and in a more private place, may be
induced, by some respectful inquiries respecting
the old style of music, to sing a song composed
by Mr. Oswald or Mr. Lampe, such as—

> " Chloe, by that borrow'd kiss,"

or—

> " Come, gentle god of soft repose " ;

or his wife's favourite ballad, beginning—

> " At Upton on the Hill
> There lived a happy pair."

Of course, no such exploit can take place in
the coffee-room ; but he will canvas the theory
of that matter there with you, or discuss the
weather, or the markets, or the theatres, or
the merits of " my Lord North," or " my Lord
Rockingham " ; for he rarely says simply lord ;
it is generally " my lord," trippingly and
genteelly off the tongue. If alone after
dinner, his great delight is the newspaper ;
which he prepares to read by wiping his
spectacles, carefully adjusting them on his
eyes, and drawing the candle close to him, so
as to stand sideways betwixt his ocular aim
and the small type. He then holds the paper
at arm's-length, and, dropping his eyelids
half down and his mouth half open, takes
cognizance of the day's information. If he
leaves off, it is only when the door is opened
by a new-comer, or when he suspects somebody is over-anxious to get the paper out of
his hand. On these occasions, he gives an
important " hem ! " or so, and resumes.

In the evening, our Old Gentleman is fond
of going to the theatre, or of having a game of
cards. If he enjoys the latter at his own house
or lodgings, he likes to play with some friends

whom he has known for many years ; but an elderly stranger may be introduced, if quiet and scientific, and the privilege is extended to younger men of letters, who, if ill players, are good losers. Not that he is a miser ; but to win money at cards is like proving his victory by getting the baggage, and to win of a younger man is a substitute for his not being able to beat him at rackets. He breaks up early, whether at home or abroad.

At the theatre, he likes a front row in the pit. He comes early, if he can do so without getting into a squeeze, and sits patiently waiting for the drawing up of the curtain, with his hands placidly lying, one over the other, on the top of his stick. He generously admires some of the best performers, but thinks them far inferior to Garrick, Woodward, and Clive. During splendid scenes he is anxious that the little boy should see.

He has been induced to look in at Vauxhall again, but likes it still less than he did years back, and cannot bear it in comparison with Ranelagh. He thinks everything looks poor, flaring, and jaded. " Ah ! " says he, with a sort of triumphant sigh, " Ranelagh was a noble place ! Such taste, such elegance, such beauty ! There was the Duchess of A., the finest woman in England, sir ; and Mrs. L., a mighty fine creature ; and Lady Susan

LEIGH HUNT

What's-her-name, that had that unfortunate affair with Sir Charles. Sir, they came swimming by you like the swans."

The Old Gentleman is very particular in having his slippers ready for him at the fire when he comes home. He is also extremely choice in his snuff, and delights to get a fresh boxful in Tavistock Street, on his way to the theatre. His box is a curiosity from India. He calls favourite young ladies by their Christian names, however slightly acquainted with them, and has a privilege also of saluting all brides, mothers, and indeed every species of lady, on the least holiday occasion. If the husband, for instance, has met with a piece of luck, he instantly moves forward, and gravely kisses the wife on the cheek. The wife then says, "My niece, sir, from the country"; and he kisses the niece. The niece, seeing her cousin biting her lips at the joke, says, "My cousin Harriet, sir"; and he kisses the cousin. He never recollects such weather, except during the Great Frost, or when he rode down with Jack Skrimshire to Newmarket. He grows young again in his little grandchildren, especially the one which he thinks most like himself, which is the handsomest. Yet he likes best, perhaps, the one most resembling his wife, and will sit with him on his lap, holding his hand in

204

silence, for a quarter of an hour together. He plays most tricks with the former, and makes him sneeze. He asks little boys in general who was the father of Zebedee's children. If his grandsons are at school, he often goes to see them, and makes them blush by telling the master or the upper scholars that they are fine boys, and of a precocious genius. He is much struck when an old acquaintance dies, but adds that he lived too fast, and that poor Bob was a sad dog in his youth—" a very sad dog, sir, mightily set upon a short life and a merry one."

When he gets very old indeed, he will sit for whole evenings, and say little or nothing ; but informs you that there is Mrs. Jones (the housekeeper)—" *She'll* talk."

WILLIAM MAKEPEACE THACKERAY

[1811–1863]

DE FINIBUS

WHEN Swift was in love with Stella, and despatching her a letter from London thrice a month by the Irish packet, you may remember how he would begin letter No. XXIII., we will say, on the very day when XXII. had been sent away, stealing out of the coffee-house or the assembly so as to be able to prattle with his dear ; " never letting go her kind hand, as it were," as some commentator or other has said in speaking of the Dean and his amour. When Mr. Johnson, walking to Dodsley's, and touching the posts in Pall Mall as he walked, forgot to pat the head of one of them, he went back and imposed his hands on it,—impelled I know not by what superstition. I have this I hope not dangerous mania too. As soon as a piece of work is out of hand, and before going to sleep, I like to begin another : it may be to write only half-a-dozen lines : but that

DE FINIBUS

is something towards Number the Next. The printer's boy has not yet reached Green Arbour Court with the copy. Those people who were alive half an hour since, Pendennis, Clive Newcome, and (what do you call him ? what was the name of the last hero ? I remember now !) Philip Firmin, have hardly drunk their glass of wine, and the mammas have only this minute got the children's cloaks on, and have been bowed out of my premises—and here I come back to the study again : *tamem usque recurro.* How lonely it looks now all these people are gone ! My dear good friends, some folks are utterly tired of you, and say, " What a poverty of friends the man has ! He is always asking us to meet those Pendennises, Newcomes, and so forth. Why does he not introduce us to some new characters ? Why is he not thrilling like Twostars, learned and profound like Three-stars, exquisitely humourous and human like Fourstars ? Why, finally, is he not somebody else ? " My good people, it is not only impossible to please you all, but it is absurd to try. The dish which one man devours, another dislikes. Is the dinner of to-day not to your taste ? Let us hope to-morrow's entertainment will be more agreeable. * * I resume my original subject. What an odd, pleasant, humourous, melancholy feeling it is to sit in the study, alone and quiet, now all these people are gone who have been boarding and lodging with me for twenty months! They have interrupted my rest : they have plagued me at all sorts of minutes : they have thrust themselves upon me when I was ill, or wished to be idle, and I have growled out a " Be hanged to you, can't you leave me alone now ? " Once or twice they have prevented my going out to dinner. Many and many a time they have prevented my coming home, because I knew they were there waiting in the study, and a plague take them ! and I have left home and family, and gone to dine at the Club, and told nobody where I went. They have bored me, those people. They have plagued me at all sorts of uncomfortable hours. They have made such a disturbance in my mind and house, that sometimes I have hardly known what was going on in my family, and scarcely have heard what my neighbour said to me. They are gone at last ; and you would expect me to be at ease ? Far from it. I should almost be glad if Woolcomb would walk in and talk to me ; or Twysden reappear, take his place in that chair opposite me, and begin one of his tremendous stories.

Madmen, you know, see visions, hold conversations with, even draw the likeness of,

people invisible to you and me.   Is this making
of people out of fancy madness ? and are
novel-writers at all entitled to strait-waist-
coats ?   I often forget people's names in life ;
and in my own stories contritely own that I
make dreadful blunders regarding them ; but
I declare, my dear sir, with repects to the
personages introduced into your humble
servant's fables, I know the people utterly—
I know the sound of their voices.   A gentleman
came in to see me the other day, who was so
like the picture of Philip Firmin in Mr. Walker's
charming drawings in the *Cornhill Magazine*,
that he was quite a curiosity to me. The
same eyes, beard, shoulders, just as you
have seen them from month to month.   Well,
he is not like the Philip Firmin in my mind.
Asleep, asleep in the grave, lies the bold, the
generous, the reckless, the tender-hearted
creature whom I have made to pass through
those adventures which have just been brought
to an end.   It is years since I heard the
laughter ringing, or saw the bright blue eyes.
When I knew him both were young.   I
become young as I think of him.   And this
morning he was alive again in this room,
ready to laugh, to fight, to weep.   As I write,
do you know, it is the grey of evening ;
the house is quiet ; everybody is out ; the
room is getting a little dark, and I look rather

WILLIAM MAKEPEACE THACKERAY

wistfully up from the paper with perhaps ever
so little fancy that HE MAY COME IN.—No ?
No movement,   No grey shade, growing more
palpable, out of which at last look the well-
known eyes.   No, the printer came and took
him away with the last page of the proofs.
And with the printer's boy did the whole
cortège of ghosts flit away, invisible ?   Ha !
stay ! what is this ?   Angels and ministers of
grace !   The door opens, and a dark form—
enters, bearing a black—a black suit of
clothes.   It is John.   He says it is time to
dress for dinner.

*   *   *   *   *

Every man who has had his German tutor,
and has been coached through the famous
" Faust " of Goethe (thou wert my instructor,
good old Weissenborn, and these eyes beheld
the great master himself in dear little Weimar
town !) has read those charming verses which
are prefixed to the drama, in which the poet
reverts to the time when his work was first
composed, and recalls the friends now departed,
who once listened to his song.   The dear
shadows rise up around him, he says ;   he lives
in the past again.   It is to-day which appears
vague and visionary.   We humbler writers
cannot create Fausts, or raise up monumental
works that shall endure for all ages ;   but our

210

books are diaries, in which our own feelings must of necessity be set down. As we look to the page written last month, or ten years ago, we remember the day and its events : the child ill, mayhap, in the adjoining room, and the doubts and fears which racked the brain as it still pursued its work ; the dear old friend who read the commencement of the tale, and whose gentle hand shall be laid in ours no more. I own for my part that, in reading pages which this hand penned formerly, I often lose sight of the text under my eyes. It is not the words I see ; but that past day ; that bygone page of life's history ; that tragedy, comedy it may be, which our little home company was enacting ; that merry-making which we shared ; that funeral which we followed ; that bitter, bitter grief which we buried.

And, such being the state of my mind, I pray gentle readers to deal kindly with their humble servant's manifold short-comings, blunders, and slips of memory. As sure as I read a page of my own composition, I find a fault or two, half-a-dozen. Jones is called Brown. Brown, who is dead, is brought to life. Aghast, and months after the number was printed, I saw that I had called Philip Firmin, Clive Newcome. Now Clive Newcome is the hero of another story by the reader's

most obedient writer. The two men are as
different in my mind's eye, as—Lord Palmers-
ton and Mr. Disraeli let us say. But there is
that blunder at page 990, line 76, volume 84
of the *Cornhill Magazine*, and it is past mending; and I wish in my life I had made no
worse blunders or errors than that which is
hereby acknowledged.

Another Finis written. Another mile-stone
passed on this journey from birth to the
next world! Sure it is a subject for solemn
cogitation. Shall we continue this story-
telling business and be voluble to the end of
our age? Will it not be presently time,
O prattler, to hold your tongue, and let
younger people speak? I have a friend, a
painter, who, like other persons who shall be
nameless, is growing old. He has never
painted with such laborious finish as his works
now show. This master is still the most
humble and diligent of scholars. Of Art, his
mistress, he is always an eager, reverent pupil.
In his calling, in yours, in mine, industry and
humility will help and comfort us. A word
with you. In a pretty large experience, I
have not found the men who write books
superior in wit or learning to those who don't
write at all. In regard of mere information,
non-writers must often be superior to writers.
You don't expect a lawyer in full practice to

be conversant with all kinds of literature ; he
is too busy with his law ; and so a writer is
commonly too busy with his own books to be
able to bestow attention on the works of other
people. After a day's work (in which I have
been depicting, let us say, the agonies of
Louisa on parting with the Captain, or the
atrocious behaviour of the wicked Marquis to
Lady Emily) I march to the Club, proposing
to improve my mind and keep myself " posted
up," as the Americans phrase is, with the
literature of the day. And what happens ?
Given, a walk after luncheon, a pleasing book,
and a most comfortable arm-chair by the fire,
and you know the rest. A doze ensues.
Pleasing book drops suddenly, is picked up
once with an air of some confusion, is laid
presently softly in lap : head falls on comfortable arm-chair cushion : eyes close : soft
nasal music is heard. Am I telling Club
secrets ? Of afternoons, after lunch, I say,
scores of sensible fogies have a doze. Perhaps
I have fallen asleep over that very book to
which " Finis " has just been written. " And
if the writer sleeps, what happens to the
readers ? " says Jones, coming down upon me
with his lightning wit. What ? You *did*
sleep over it ? And a very good thing too.
These eyes have more than once seen a friend
dozing over pages which this hand has written.

WILLIAM MAKEPEACE THACKERAY

There is a vignette somewhere in one of my
books of a friend so caught napping with
" Pendennis," or the " Newcomes," in his
lap ; and if a writer can give you a sweet,
soothing, harmless sleep, has he not done you
a kindness ? So is the author who excites
and interests you worthy of your thanks and
benedictions. I am troubled with fever
and ague, that seizes me at odd intervals and
prostrates me for a day. There is cold fit, for
which, I am thankful to say, hot brandy-and-
water is prescribed, and this induces hot fit,
and so on. In one or two of these fits I have
read novels with the most fearful contentment
of mind. Once, on the Mississippi, it was my
dearly beloved " Jacob Faithful " ; once at
Frankfort O.M., the delightful " Vingt Ans
Après " of Monsieur Dumas : once at Tun-
bridge Wells, the thrilling " Woman in
White " ; and these books gave me amusement
from morning till sunset. I remember those
ague fits with a great deal of pleasure and
gratitude. Think of a whole day in bed,
and a good novel for a companion ! No cares :
no remorse about idleness : no visitors : and
the Woman in White or the Chevalier d'Artagan
to tell me stories from dawn to night !
" Please, ma'am, my master's compliments,
and can he have the third volume ? " (This
message was sent to an astonished friend and

neighbour, who lent me, volume by volume, the *W. in W.*). How do you like your novels ? I like mine strong, " hot with," and no mistake : no love-making : no observations about society : little dialogue, except where the characters are bullying each other : plenty of fighting : and a villain in the cupboard, who is to suffer tortures just before Finis. I don't like your melancholy Finis. I never read the history of a consumptive heroine twice. If I might give a short hint to an impartial writer (as the *Examiner* used to say in old days), it would be to act, *not* à la mode le pays de Pole (I think that was the phraseology), but *always* to give quarter. In the story of Philip, just come to an end, I have the permission of the author to state that he was going to drown the two villains of the piece—a certain Doctor F—— and a certain Mr. T. M—— on board the " President," or some other tragic ship—but you see I relented. I pictured to myself Firmin's ghastly face amid the crowd of shuddering people on that reeling deck in the lonely ocean, and thought, " Thou ghastly lying wretch, thou shalt not be drowned : thou shalt have a fever only ; a knowledge of thy danger ; and a chance— ever so small a chance—of repentance." I wonder whether he *did* repent when he found himself in the yellow-fever, in Virginia ?

WILLIAM MAKEPEACE THACKERAY

The probability is, he fancied that his son had injured him very much, and forgave him on his deathbed. Do you imagine there is a great deal of genuine right-down remorse in the world ? Don't people rather find excuses which make their minds easy ; endeavour to prove to themselves that they have been lamentably belied and misunderstood ; and try and forgive the persecutors who *will* present that bill when it is due ; and not bear malice against the cruel ruffian who takes them to the police-office for stealing the spoons ? Years ago I had a quarrel with a certain well-known person (I believed a statement regarding him which his friends imparted to me, and which turned out to be quite incorrect). To his dying day that quarrel was never quite made up. I said to his brother, " Why is your brother's soul still dark against me ? it is I who ought to be angry and unforgiving : for I was in the wrong." In the region which they now inhabit (for Finis has been set to the volumes of the lives of both here below), if they take any cognizance of our squabbles, and tittle-tattles, and gossips on earth here, I hope they admit that my little error was not of a nature unpardonable. If you have never committed a worse, my good sir, surely the score against you will not be heavy. Ha, *dilectissimi fratres !* It is in regard of sins *not* found out that we may say or sing (in an under-tone, in a most penitent and lugubrious minor key), *Miserere nobis miseris peccatoribus.*

Among the sins of commission which novel-writers not seldom perpetrate, is the sin of grandiloquence, or tall-talking, against which, for my part, I will offer up a special *libera me.* This is the sin of schoolmasters, governesses, critics, sermoners, and instructors of young or old people. Nay (for I am making a clean breast, and liberating my soul), perhaps of all the novel-spinners now extant, the present speaker is the most addicted to preaching. Does he not stop perpetually in his story and begin to preach to you ? When he ought to be engaged with business, is he not for ever taking the Muse by the sleeve, and plaguing her with some of his cynical sermons ? I cry *peccavi* loudly and heartily. I tell you I would like to be able to write a story which should show no egotism whatever—in which there should be no reflections, no cynicism, no vulgarity (and so forth), but an incident in every other page, a villain, a battle, a mystery in every chapter. I should like to be able to feed a reader so spicily as to leave him hungering and thirsting for more at the end of every monthly meal.

Alexandre Dumas describes himself, when inventing the plan of a work, as lying silent on

his back for two whole days on the deck of a
yacht in a Mediterranean port. At the end of
the two days he arose and called for dinner.
In those two days he had built his plot. He
had moulded a mighty clay, to be cast presently
in perennial brass. The chapters, the characters, the incidents, the combinations were all
arranged in the artist's brain ere he set a pen
to paper. My Pegasus won't fly, so as to let
me survey the field below me. He has no
wings, he is blind of one eye certainly, he is
restive, stubborn, slow; crops a hedge when
he ought to be galloping, or gallops when he
ought to be quiet. He never will show off when
I want him. Sometimes he goes at a pace
which surprises me. Sometimes, when I most
wish him to make the running, the brute turns
restive, and I am obliged to let him take his
own time. I wonder do other novel-writers
experience this fatalism? They *must* go a
certain way, in spite of themselves. I have
been surprised at the observations made by
some of my characters. It seems as if an occult
Power was moving the pen. The personage
does or says something, and I ask, how the
dickens did he come to think of that? Every
man has remarked in dreams, the vast dramatic
power which is sometimes evinced; I won't say
the surprising power, for nothing does surprise
you in dreams. But those strange characters

you meet make instant observations of which
you never can have thought previously. In
like manner, the imagination foretells things.
We spake anon of the inflated style of some
writers. What also if there is an *afflated* style—
when a writer is like a Pythoness on her oracle
tripod, and mighty words, words which he cannot help, come blowing and bellowing, and
whistling, and moaning through the speaking
pipes of his bodily organ ? I have told you it
was a very queer shock to me the other day
when, with a letter of introduction in his hand,
the artist's (not my) Philip Firmin walked into
this room, and sat down in the chair opposite.
In the novel of " Pendennis," written ten years
ago, there is an account of a certain Costigan,
whom I had invented (as I suppose authors
invent their personages out of scraps, heel-
taps, odds and ends of characters). I was
smoking in a tavern parlour one night—and
this Costigan came into the room alive—the
very man :—the most remarkable resemblance
of the printed sketches of the man, of the rude
drawings in which I had depicted him. He
had the same little coat, the same battered hat,
cocked on one eye, the same twinkle in that
eye. " Sir," said I, knowing him to be an old
friend whom I had met in unknown regions,
" sir," I said, " may I offer you a glass of
brandy-and-water ? " " *Bedad, ye may,*" says

he, " *and I'll sing ye a song tu.*" Of course he
spoke with an Irish brogue. Of course he had
been in the army. In ten minutes he pulled
out an Army Agent's account, whereon his
name was written. A few months after we
read of him in a police court. How had I
come to know him, to divine him ? Nothing
shall convince me that I have not seen that
man in the world of spirits. In the world of
spirits and water I know I did : but that is a
mere quibble of words. I was not surprised
when he spoke in an Irish brogue. I had had
cognizance of him before somehow. Who has
not felt that little shock which arises when a
person, a place, some words in a book (there is
always a collocation) present themselves to you,
and you know that you have before met the
same person, words, scene, and so forth ?

They used to call the good Sir Walter the
" Wizard of the North." What if some writer
should appear who can write so *enchantingly*
that he shall be able to call into actual life the
people whom he invents ? What if Mignon,
and Margaret, and Goetz von Berlichingen are
alive now (though I don't say they are visible),
and Dugald Dalgetty and Ivanhoe were to step
in at that open window by the little garden
yonder ? Suppose Uncas and our noble old
Leather Stocking were to glide silent in ?
Suppose Athos, Porthos and Aramis should

enter with a noiseless swagger, curling their
moustaches ? And dearest Amelia Booth, on
Uncle Toby's arm ; and Tittlebat Titmouse,
with his hair dyed green ; and all the Crummles
company of comedians, with the Gil Blas troop ;
and Sir Roger de Coverley ; and the greatest
of all crazy gentlemen, the Knight of La
Mancha, with his blessed squire ?   I say to you,
I look rather wistfully towards the window,
musing upon these people.   Were any of them
to enter, I think I should not be very much
frightened.   Dear old friends, what pleasant
hours I have had with them !   We do not see
each other very often, but when we do, we are
ever happy to meet.   I had a capital half hour
with Jacob Faithful last night ; when the
last sheet was corrected, when " Finis " had
been written, and the printer's boy, with the
copy, was safe in Green Arbour Court.
   So you are gone, little printer's boy, with the
last scratches and corrections on the proof, and
a fine flourish by way of Finis at the story's
end.   The last corrections ?   I say those last
corrections seem never to be finished.   A plague
upon the weeds ! Every day, when I walk in
my own little literary garden-plot, I spy some,
and should like to have a spud, and root them
out.   Those idle words, neighbour, are past
remedy.   That turning back to the old pages
produces anything but elation of mind.   Would

you not pay a pretty fine to be able to cancel
some of them ?   Oh, the sad old pages, the dull
old pages ! Oh, the cares, the *ennui*, the
squabbles, the repetitions, the old conversations
over and over again ! But now and again a
kind thought is recalled, and now and again a
dear memory.   Yet a few chapters more, and
then the last : after which, behold Finis itself
come to an end, and the Infinite begun.

ALEXANDER SMITH

[1830–1867]

A LARK'S FLIGHT

RIGHTLY or wrongly, during the last twenty or thirty years a strong feeling has grown up in the public mind against the principle, and a still stronger feeling against the practice, of capital punishments. Many people who will admit that the execution of the murderer may be, abstractly considered, just enough, sincerely doubt whether such execution be expedient, and are in their own minds perfectly certain that it cannot fail to demoralise the spectators. In consequence of this, executions have become rare; and it is quite clear that many scoundrels, well worthy of the noose, contrive to escape it. When, on the occasion of a wretch being turned off, the spectators are few, it is remarked by the newspapers that the mob is beginning to lose its proverbial cruelty, and to be stirred by humane pulses; when they are numerous, and especially when girls and women form a majority, the circumstance

223

is noticed and deplored. It is plain enough
that, if the newspaper considered such an
exhibition beneficial, it would not lament over
a few thousand eager witnesses : if the sermon
be edifying, you cannot have too large a
congregation ; if you teach a moral lesson in a
grand, impressive way, it is difficult to see how
you can have too many pupils. Of course,
neither the justice nor the expediency of capital
punishments falls to be discussed here. This,
however, may be said, that the popular feeling
against them may not be so admirable a proof
of enlightenment as many believe. It is true
that the spectacle is painful, horrible ; but in
pain and horror there is often hidden a certain
salutariness, and the repulsion of which we are
conscious is as likely to arise from debilitation
of public nerve, as from a higher reach of public
feeling. To my own thinking, it is out of this
pain and hatefulness that an execution becomes
invested with an ideal grandeur. It is sheer
horror to all concerned—sheriffs, halbertmen,
chaplain, spectators, Jack Ketch, and culprit ;
but out of all this, and towering behind the
vulgar and hideous accessories of the scaffold,
gleams the majesty of implacable law. When
every other fine morning a dozen cut-purses
were hanged at Tyburn, and when such sights
did not run very strongly against the popular
current, the spectacle *was* vulgar, and could be

of use only to the possible cut-purses congregated around the foot of the scaffold. Now,
when the law has become so far merciful ; when
the punishment of death is reserved for the
murderer ; when he can be condemned only on
the clearest evidence ; when, as the days draw
slowly on to doom, the frightful event impend-
ing over one stricken wretch throws its
shadow over the heart of every man, woman,
and child in the great city ; and when the
official persons whose duty it is to see the
letter of the law carried out perform that duty
at the expense of personal pain—a public
execution is not vulgar, it becomes positively
sublime. It is dreadful, of course ; but its
dreadfulness melts into pure awfulness. The
attention is taken off the criminal, and is lost
in a sense of the grandeur of justice ; and the
spectator who beholds an execution, solely as
it appears to the eye, without recognition of
the idea which towers behind it, must be a very
unspiritual and unimaginative spectator indeed.

It is taken for granted that the spectators of
public executions—the artisans and country
people who take up their stations overnight as
close to the barriers as possible, and the
wealthier classes who occupy hired windows
and employ opera-glasses—are merely drawn
together by a morbid relish for horrible sights.
He is a bold man who will stand forward as

the advocate of such persons—so completely
is the popular mind made up as to their tastes
and motives. It is not disputed that the large
body of the mob, and of the occupants at windows, have been drawn together by an appetite
for excitement ; but it is quite possible that
many come there from an impulse altogether
different. Just consider the nature of the
expected sight—a man in tolerable health
probably, in possession of all his faculties,
perfectly able to realise his position, conscious
that for him this world and the next are so
near that only a few seconds divide them—
such a man stands in the seeing of several
thousand eyes. He is so peculiarly circum-
stanced, so utterly lonely—hearing the tolling
of his own death-bell, yet living, wearing the
mourning clothes for his own funeral, that he
holds the multitude together by a shuddering
fascination. The sight is a peculiar one, you
must admit, and every peculiarity has its
attractions. Your volcano is more attractive
than your ordinary mountain. Then consider
the unappeasable curiosity as to death which
haunts every human being, and how pathetic
that curiosity is, in so far as it suggests our own
ignorance and helplessness, and we see at once
that people *may* flock to public executions for
other purposes than the gratification of morbid
tastes : that they would pluck if they could

some little knowledge of what death is ; that imaginatively they attempt to reach to it, to touch and handle it through an experience which is not their own. It is some obscure desire of this kind, a movement of curiosity not altogether ignoble, but in some degree pathetic ; some rude attempt of the imagination to wrest from the death of the criminal information as to the great secret in which each is profoundly interested, which draws around the scaffold people from the country harvest-fields, and from the streets and alleys of the town. Nothing interests men so much as death. Age cannot wither it, nor custom stale it. " A greater crowd would come to see me hanged," Cromwell is reported to have said when the populace came forth on a public occasion. The Lord Protector was right in a sense of which, perhaps, at the moment he was not aware. Death is greater than official position. When a man has to die, he may safely dispense with stars and ribbands. He is invested with a greater dignity than is held in the gift of kings. A greater crowd *would* have gathered to see Cromwell hanged, but the compliment would have been paid to death rather than to Cromwell. Never were the motions of Charles I so scrutinised as when he stood for a few moments on the scaffold that winter morning at Whitehall. King Louis was no great orator usually, but when on the 2nd January, 1793, he attempted to speak a few words in the Place de la Revolution, it was found necessary to drown his voice in a harsh roll of soldiers' drums. Not without a meaning do people come forth to see men die. We stand in the valley, they on the hill-top, and on their faces strikes the light of the other world, and from some sign or signal of theirs we attempt to discover or extract a hint of what it is all like.

To be publicly put to death, for whatever reason, must ever be a serious matter. It is always bitter, but there are degrees in its bitterness. It is easy to die like Stephen with an opened heaven above you, crowded with angel faces. It is easy to die like Balmerino with a chivalrous sigh for the White Rose, and an audible " God bless King James." Such men die for a cause in which they glory, and are supported thereby ; they are conducted to the portals of the next world by the angels, Faith, Pity, Admiration. But it is not easy to die in expiation of a crime like murder, which engirdles you with trembling and horror even in the loneliest places, which cuts you off from the sympathies of your kind, which reduces the universe to two elements—a sense of personal identity, and a memory of guilt. In so dying, there must be inconceivable bitterness ; a man can have no other support than what

strength he may pluck from despair, or from
the iron with which nature may have originally
braced heart and nerve. Yet, taken as a whole,
criminals on the scaffold comport themselves
creditably. They look Death in the face when
he wears his cruellest aspect, and if they flinch
somewhat, they can at least bear to look. I
cannot believe that, for the criminal, execution
within the prison walls, with no witnesses save
some half-dozen official persons, would be
infinitely more terrible than execution in the
presence of a curious, glaring mob. The daylight and the publicity are alien elements,
which wean the man a little from himself. He
steadies his dizzy brain on the crowd beneath
and around him. He has his last part to play,
and his manhood rallies to play it well. Nay,
so subtly is vanity intertwined with our
motives, the noblest and the most ignoble,
that I can fancy a poor wretch with the noose
dangling at his ear, and with barely five minutes
to live, soothed somewhat with the idea that
his firmness and composure will earn him the
approbation, perhaps the pity, of the spectators. He would take with him, if he could, the
good opinion of his fellows. This composure of
criminals puzzles one. Have they looked at
death so long and closely that familiarity has
robbed it of terror ? Has life treated them so
harshly, that they are tolerably well pleased to

be quit of it on any terms ? Or is the whole
thing mere blind stupor and delirium, in which
thought is paralysed, and the man an auto-
maton ? Speculation is useless. The fact
remains that criminals for the most part die
well and bravely. It is said that the champion-
ship of England was to be decided at some
little distance from London on the morning of
the day on which Thurtell was executed, and
that, when he came out on the scaffold, he
inquired privily of the executioner if the result
had yet become known. Jack Ketch was not
aware, and Thurtell expressed his regret that
the ceremony in which he was chief actor
should take place so inconveniently early in
the day. Think of a poor Thurtell forced to
take his long journey an hour, perhaps, before
the arrival of intelligence so important !

More than twenty years ago I saw two men
executed, and the impression then made
remains fresh to this day. For this there were
many reasons. The deed for which the men
suffered created an immense sensation. They
were hanged on the spot where the murder was
committed—on a rising ground, some four miles
north-east of the city ; and as an attempt at
rescue was apprehended, there was a considerable display of military force on the occasion.
And when, in the dead silence of thousands, the
criminals stood beneath the halters, an incident

occurred, quite natural and slight in itself, but when taken in connection with the business then proceeding, so unutterably tragic, so overwhelming in its pathetic suggestion of contrast, that the feeling of it has never departed, and never will. At the time, too, I speak of, I was very young; the world was like a die newly cut, whose every impression is fresh and vivid.

While the railway which connects two northern capitals was being built, two brothers from Ireland, named Doolan, were engaged upon it in the capacity of navvies. For some fault or negligence, one of the brothers was dismissed by the overseer—a Mr. Green—of that particular portion of the line on which they were employed. The dismissed brother went off in search of work, and the brother who remained—Dennis was the Christian name of him—brooded over this supposed wrong, and in his dull, twilighted brain revolved projects of vengeance. He did not absolutely mean to take Green's life, but he meant to thrash him within an inch of it. Dennis, anxious to thrash Green, but not quite seeing his way to it, opened his mind one afternoon, when work was over, to his friends—fellow-Irishmen and navvies —Messrs. Redding and Hickie. These took up Doolan's wrong as their own, and that evening, by the dull light of a bothy fire, they held a rude parliament, discussing ways and

means of revenge. It was arranged that
Green should be thrashed—the amount of
thrashing left an open question, to be decided,
unhappily, when the blood was up and the
cinder of rage blown into a flame. Hickie's
spirit was found not to be a mounting one,
and it was arranged that the active partners in
the game should be Doolan and Redding.
Doolan, as the aggrieved party, was to strike
the first blow, and Redding, as the aggrieved
party's particular friend, asked and obtained
permission to strike the second. The main
conspirators, with a fine regard for the feelings
of the weaker Hickie, allowed him to provide
the weapons of assault—so that by some slight
filament of aid he might connect himself with
the good cause. The unambitious Hickie at
once applied himself to his duty. He went out,
and in due time returned with two sufficient iron
pokers. The weapons were examined, approved
of, and carefully laid aside. Doolan, Redding,
and Hickie ate their suppers, and retired to their
several couches to sleep, peacefully enough no
doubt. About the same time, too, Green, the
English overseer, threw down his weary limbs,
and entered on his last sleep—little dreaming
what the morning had in store for him.

Uprose the sun, and uprose Doolan and
Redding, and dressed, and thrust each his
sufficient iron poker up the sleeve of his

blouse, and went forth. They took up their station on a temporary wooden bridge which spanned the line, and waited there. Across the bridge, as was expected, did Green ultimately come. He gave them good morning; asked, " why they were loafing about ? " received no very pertinent answer, perhaps did not care to receive one; whistled—the unsuspecting man! —thrust his hands into his breeches pockets, turned his back on them, and leaned over the railing of the bridge, inspecting the progress of the works beneath. The temptation was really too great. What could wild Irish flesh and blood do ? In a moment out from the sleeve of Doolan's blouse came the hidden poker, and the first blow was struck, bringing Green to the ground. The friendly Redding, who had bargained for the second, and who, naturally enough, was in fear of being cut out altogether, jumped on the prostrate man, and fulfilled his share of the bargain with a will. It was Redding it was supposed who sped the unhappy Green. They overdid their work—like young authors—giving many more blows than were sufficient, and then fled. The works, of course, were that morning in consternation. Redding and Hickie were, if I remember rightly, apprehended in the course of the day. Doolan got off, leaving no trace of his whereabouts.

These particulars were all learned sub-
sequently. The first intimation which we
schoolboys received of anything unusual
having occurred, was the sight of a detach-
ment of soldiers with fixed bayonets, trousers
rolled up over muddy boots, marching past
the front of the Cathedral hurriedly home to
barracks. This was a circumstance somewhat unusual. We had, of course, frequently
seen a couple of soldiers trudging along with
sloped muskets, and that cruel glitter of steel
which no one of us could look upon quite
unmoved ; but in such cases, the deserter
walking between them in his shirt-sleeves,
his pinioned hands covered from public gaze
by the loose folds of his great-coat, explained
everything. But from the hurried march
of these mud-splashed men, nothing could
be gathered, and we were left to speculate
upon its meaning. Gradually, however, before the evening fell, the rumour of a murder
having been committed spread through the
city, and with that I instinctively connected
the apparition of the file of muddy soldiers.
Next day, murder was in every mouth. My
school-fellows talked of it to the detriment
of their lessons ; it flavoured the tobacco
of the fustian artisan as he smoked to work
after breakfast ; it walked on 'Change amongst
the merchants. It was known that two of

the persons implicated had been captured,
but that the other, the guiltiest, was still
at large; and in a few days out on every
piece of boarding and blank wall came the
" Hue and cry "—describing Doolan like a
photograph, to the colour and cut of his
whiskers, and offering a £100 as reward for
his apprehension—like a silent, implacable
bloodhound following close on the track of
the murderer. This terrible broadsheet I
read, was certain that *he* had read it also,
and fancy ran riot over the ghastly fact.
For him no hope, no rest, no peace, no touch
of hands gentler than the hangman's; all
the world is after him like a roaring prairie
of flame! I thought of Doolan, weary, foot-
sore, heart-sore, entering some quiet village
of an evening; and to quench his thirst,
going up to the public well, around which the
gossips are talking, and hearing that they were
talking of *him*; and seeing from the well
itself IT glaring upon him, as if conscious of
his presence, with a hundred eyes of vengeance.
I thought of him asleep in out-houses, and starting up in wild dreams of the policeman's hand
upon his shoulder fifty times ere morning. He had
committed the crime of Cain, and the weird of
Cain he had to endure. But yesterday innocent,
how unimportant; to-day bloody-handed, the
whole world is talking of him, and everything

ALEXANDER SMITH

he touches, the very bed he sleeps on, steals
from him his secret, and is eager to betray !

Doolan was finally captured in Liverpool,
and in the Spring Assize the three men were
brought to trial. The jury found them
guilty, but recommended Hickie to mercy
on account of some supposed weakness of
mind on his part. Sentence was, of course,
pronounced with the usual solemnities. They
were set apart to die ; and when snug abed o'
nights—for imagination is most mightily moved
by contrast—I crept into their desolate hearts,
and tasted a misery which was not my own.
As already said, Hickie was recommended
to mercy, and the recommendation was
ultimately in the proper quarter given effect to.

The evening before the execution has
arrived, and the reader has now to imagine
the early May sunset falling pleasantly on the
outskirts of the city. The houses looking
out upon an open square or space, have little
plots of garden-ground in their fronts, in
which mahogany-coloured wall-flowers and
mealy auriculas are growing. The side of the
square, along which the City Road stretches
northward, is occupied by a blind-asylum,
a brick building, the bricks painted red and
picked out with white, after the tidy English
fashion, and a high white cemetery wall, over
which peers the spire of the Gothic Cathedral ;

236

A LARK'S FLIGHT

and beyond that, on the other side of the
ravine, rising out of the populous city of the
dead, a stone John Knox looks on the Cathedral, a Bible clutched in his outstretched
and menacing hand. On all this the May
sunset is striking, dressing everything in its
warm, pleasant pink, lingering in the tufts
of foliage that nestle around the asylum,
and dipping the building itself one half in
light, one half in tender shade. This open
space or square is an excellent place for the
games of us boys, and " Prisoner's Base " is
being carried out with as much earnestness
as the business of life now by those of us who
are left. The girls, too, have their games
of a quiet kind, which we held in huge scorn
and contempt. In two files, linked arm-in-
arm, they alternately dance towards each
other and then retire, singing the while, in
their clear, girlish treble, verses, the meaning
and pertinence of which time has worn away—

"The Campsie Duke's a-riding, a-riding, a-riding,"

being the oft-recurring " owercome," or
refrain. All this is going on in the pleasant
sunset light, when by the apparition of certain
waggons coming up from the city, piled
high with blocks and beams, and guarded
by a dozen dragoons, on whose brazen helmets
the sunset danced, every game is dismembered,

237

and we are in a moment a mere mixed mob
of boys and girls, flocking around to stare
and wonder. Just at this place something
went wrong with one of the waggon wheels,
and the procession came to a stop. A crowd
collected, and we heard some of the grown-up
people say, that the scaffold was being carried
out for the ceremony of to-morrow. Then,
more intensely than ever, one realised the
condition of the doomed men. *We* were at
our happy games in the sunset, *they* were
entering on their last night on earth. After
hammering and delay the wheel was put to
rights, the sunset died out, waggons and
dragoons got into motion and disappeared;
and all the night through, whether awake or
asleep, I saw the torches burning, and heard
the hammers clinking, and witnessed as
clearly as if I had been an onlooker, the
horrid structure rising, till it stood complete,
with a huge cross-beam from which two
empty halters hung, in the early morning light.

Next morning the whole city was in
commotion. Whether the authorities were
apprehensive that a rescue would be attempted,
or were anxious merely to strike terror into
the hundreds of wild Irishry engaged on the
railway, I cannot say : in any case, there was
a display of military force quite unusual.
The carriage in which the criminals—Catholics

both—and their attendant priests were seated, was guarded by soldiers with fixed bayonets; indeed, the whole regiment then lying in the city was massed in front and behind, with a cold, frightful glitter of steel. Besides the foot soldiers, there were dragoons, and two pieces of cannon; a whole little army, in fact. With a slenderer force battles have been won which have made a mark in history. What did the prisoners think of their strange importance, and of the tramp and hurly-burly all around? When the procession moved out of the city, it seemed to draw with it almost the entire population; and when once the country roads were reached, the crowds spread over the fields on either side, ruthlessly treading down the tender wheat braird. I got a glimpse of the doomed, blanched faces which had haunted me so long, at the turn of the road, where, for the first time, the black cross-beam with its empty halters first became visible to them. Both turned and regarded it with a long, steady look; that done, they again bent their heads attentively to the words of the clergyman. I suppose in that long, eager, fascinated gaze they practically *died*—that for them death had no additional bitterness. When the mound was reached on which the scaffold stood, there was immense confusion. Around

it a wide space was kept clear by the military ;
the cannon were placed in position ; out
flashed the swords of the dragoons ; beneath
and around on every side was the crowd.
Between two brass helmets I could see the
scaffold clearly enough, and when in a little
while the men, bareheaded and with their
attendants, appeared upon it, the surging
crowd became stiffened with fear and awe.
And now it was that the incident so simple,
so natural, so much in the ordinary course
of things, and yet so frightful in its tragic
suggestions, took place. Be it remembered
that the season was early May, that the day
was fine, that the wheat-fields were clothing
themselves in the green of the young crop,
and that around the scaffold, standing on a
sunny mound, a wide space was kept clear.
When the men appeared beneath the beam,
each under his proper halter, there was a
dead silence—everyone was gazing too intently
to whisper to his neighbour even. Just then,
out of the grassy space at the foot of the
scaffold, in the dead silence audible to all,
a lark rose from the side of its nest, and went
singing upwards in its happy flight. O
heaven ! How did that song translate itself into
dying ears ? Did it bring, in one wild burning
moment, father and mother, and poor Irish
cabin, and prayers said at bed-time, and the

smell of turf fires, and innocent sweethearting, and rising and setting suns ? Did it—but the dragoon's horse has become restive, and his brass helmet bobs up and down and blots everything ; and there is a sharp sound, and I feel the great crowd heave and swing, and hear it torn by a sharp shiver of pity, and the men whom I saw so near but a moment ago are at immeasurable distance, and have solved the great enigma—and the lark has not yet finished his flight : you can see and hear him yonder in the fringe of a white May cloud.

This ghastly lark's flight, when the circumstances are taken into consideration, is, I am inclined to think, more terrible than anything of the same kind which I have encountered in books. The artistic use of contrast as background and accompaniment, are well known to nature and the poets. Joy is continually worked on sorrow, sorrow on joy ; riot is framed in peace, peace in riot. Lear and the Fool always go together. Trafalgar is being fought while Napoleon is sitting on horseback watching the Austrian army laying down its arms at Ulm. In Hood's poem, it is when looking on the released schoolboys at their games that Eugene Aram remembers he is a murderer. And these two poor Irish labourers could not die without hearing a lark singing in their ears. It is nature's fashion.

She never quite goes along with us. She is sombre at weddings, sunny at funerals, and she frowns on ninety-nine out of a hundred picnics.

There is a stronger element of terror in this incident of the lark than in any story of a similar kind I can remember.

A good story is told of an Irish gentleman—still known in London society—who inherited the family estates and the family banshee. The estates he lost—no uncommon circumstance in the history of Irish gentlemen—but the banshee, who expected no favours, stuck to him in his adversity, and crossed the channel with him, making herself known only on occasions of death-beds and sharp family misfortunes. This gentleman had an ear, and, seated one night at the opera, the *keen*—heard once or twice before on memorable occasions—thrilled through the din of the orchestra and the passion of the singers. He hurried home, of course, found his immediate family well, but on the morrow a telegram arrived with the announcement of a brother's death. Surely of all superstitions that is the most imposing which makes the other world interested in the events which befall our mortal lot. For the mere pomp and pride of it, your ghost is worth a dozen retainers, and it is entirely inexpensive. the peculiarity and supernatural worth of

this story lies in the idea of the old wail
piercing through the sweet entanglement of
stringed instruments and extinguishing Grisi.
Modern circumstances and luxury crack, as
it were, and reveal for a moment misty and
aboriginal time big with portent. There is a
ridiculous Scotch story in which one gruesome
touch lives. A clergyman's female servant
was seated in the kitchen one Saturday night
reading the Scriptures, when she was somewhat startled by hearing at the door the tap
and voice of her sweetheart. Not expecting
him, and the hour being somewhat late, she
opened it in astonishment, and was still more
astonished to hear him on entering, abuse
Scripture-reading. He behaved altogether in
an unprecedented manner, and in many ways
terrified the poor girl. Ultimately he knelt
before her, and laid his head on her lap. You
can fancy her consternation when glancing
down she discovered that, *instead of hair,
the head was covered with the moss of the moorland.* By a sacred name she adjured him to
tell who he was, and in a moment the figure
was gone. It was the Fiend, of course—
diminished sadly since Milton saw him bridge
chaos—fallen from worlds to kitchen-wenches.
But just think how in the story, in half-pity,
in half-terror, the popular feeling of home-
lessness, of being outcast, of being unsheltered

243

as waste and desert places, has incarnated itself in that strange covering of the head. It is a true supernatural touch. One other story I have heard in the misty Hebrides : A Skye gentleman was riding along an empty moorland road. All at once, as if it had sprung from the ground, the empty road was crowded by a funeral procession. Instinctively he drew his horse to a side to let it pass, which it did without sound of voice, without tread of foot. Then he knew it was an apparition. Staring on it, he knew every person who either bore the corpse or walked behind as mourners. There were the neighbouring proprietors at whose houses he dined, there were the members of his own kirk-session, there were the men to whom he was wont to give good-morning when he met them on the road or at market. Unable to discover his own image in the throng, he was inwardly marvelling whose funeral it *could* be, when the troop of spectres vanished, and the road was empty as before. Then, remembering that the coffin had an invisible occupant, he cried out, " It is my funeral ! " and, with all his strength taken out of him, rode home to die. All these stories have their own touches of terror ; yet I am inclined to think that my lark rising from the scaffold foot, and singing to two such auditors, is more terrible than any one of them.

ROBERT LOUIS STEVENSON

[1850–1894]

THE LANTERN BEARERS*

I

THESE boys congregated every autumn about a certain easterly fisher-village, where they tasted in a high degree the glory of existence. The place was created seemingly on purpose for the diversion of young gentlemen. A street or two of houses, mostly red and many of them tiled ; a number of fine trees clustered about the manse and the kirkyard, and turning the chief street into a shady alley ; many little gardens more than usually bright with flowers ; nets a-drying, and fisher-wives scolding in the barkward parts ; a smell of fish, a genial smell of seaweed ; whiffs of blowing sand at the street corners ; shops with golf-balls and bottled lollipops ; another shop with penny pickwicks (that remarkable cigar) and

* From " Across the Plains " (Chatto & Windus).

245

the *London Journal,* dear to me for its startling
pictures, and a few novels, dear for their
suggestive names : such, as well as memory
serves me, were the ingredients of the town.
These, you are to conceive posted on a spit
between two sandy bays, and sparsely flanked
with villas—enough for the boys to lodge in
with their subsidiary parents, not enough
(not yet enough) to cocknify the scene : a
haven in the rocks in front : in front of that,
a file of grey islents : to the left, endless links
and sand wreaths, a wilderness of hiding-
holes, alive with popping rabbits and soaring
gulls : to the right, a range of seaward crags,
one rugged brow beyond another ; the ruins
of a mighty and ancient fortress on the brink
of one ; coves between—now charmed into
sunshine quiet, now whistling with wind and
clamorous with bursting surges ; the dens
and sheltered hollows redolent of thyme
and southernwood, the air at the cliff's edge
brisk and clean and pungent of the sea—in
front of all the Bass Rock, tilted seaward
like a doubtful bather, the surf ringing it with
white, the solan-geese hanging round its summit
like a great and glittering smoke. This choice
piece of seaboard was sacred, besides, to the
wrecker ; and the Bass, in the eye of fancy,
still flew the colours of King James ; and in
the ear of fancy the arches of Tantallon still

rang with horse-shoe iron, and echoed to the commands of Bell-the-Cat.

There was nothing to mar your days, if you were a boy summering in that part, but the embarrassment of pleasure. You might golf if you wanted ; but I seem to have been better employed. You might secrete yourself in the Lady's Walk, a certain sunless dingle of elders, all mossed over by the damp as green as grass, and dotted here and there by the streamside with roofless walls, the cold homes of anchorites. To fit themselves for life, and with a special eye to acquire the art of smoking, it was even common for the boys to harbour there ; and you might have seen a single penny pickwick, honestly shared in lengths with a blunt knife, bestrew the glen with these apprentices. Again, you might join our fishing parties, where we sat perched as thick as solan-geese, a covey of little anglers, boy and girl, angling over each other's heads, to the much entanglement of lines and loss of podleys and consequent shrill recrimination— shrill as the geese themselves. Indeed, had that been all, you might have done this often ; but though fishing be a fine pastime, the podley is scarce to be regarded as a dainty for the table ; and it was a point of honour that a boy should eat all that he had taken. Or again, you might climb the Law, where the whale's jawbone stood landmark in the buzzing wind, and behold the face of many counties, and the smoke and spires of many towns, and the sails of distant ships. You might bathe, now in the flaws of fine weather, that we pathetically call our summer, now in a gale of wind, with the sand scourging your bare hide, your clothes thrashing abroad from underneath their guardian stone, the froth of the great breakers casting you headlong ere it had drowned your knees. Or you might explore the tidal rocks, above all in the ebb of springs, when the very roots of the hills were for the nonce discovered ; following my leader from one group to another, groping in slippery tangle for the wreck of ships, wading in pools after the abominable creatures of the sea, and ever with an eye cast backward on the march of the tide and the menaced line of your retreat. And then you might go Crusoeing, a word that covers all extempore eating in the open air : digging perhaps a house under the margin of the links, kindling a fire of the sea-ware, and cooking apples there—if they were truly apples, for I sometimes suppose the merchant must have played us off with some inferior and quite local fruit, capable of resolving, in the neighbourhood of fire, into mere sand and smoke and iodine ; or perhaps pushing to Tantallon,

you might lunch on sandwiches and visions
in the grassy court, while the wind hummed
in the crumbling turrets; or clambering along
the coast, eat geans* (the worst, I must suppose,
in Christendom) from an adventurous gean
tree that had taken root under a cliff, where
it was shaken with an ague of east wind,
and silvered after gales with salt, and grew
so foreign among its bleak surroundings that
to eat of its produce was an adventure in
itself.

There are mingled some dismal memories
with so many that were joyous. Of the
fisher-wife, for instance, who had cut her
throat at Canty Bay; and of how I ran with
the other children to the top of the Quadrant,
and beheld a posse of silent people escorting
a cart, and on the cart, bound in a chair,
her throat bandaged, and the bandage all
bloody—horror!—the fisher-wife herself, who
continued thenceforth to hag-ride my thoughts,
and even to-day (as I recall the scene) darkens
daylight. She was lodged in the little old
jail in the chief street; but whether or no
she died there, with a wise terror of the worst,
I never inquired. She had been tippling;
it was but a dingy tragedy; and it seems
strange and hard that, after all these years,
the poor crazy sinner should be still pilloried

* Wild cherries.

on her cart in the scrap-book of my memory.
Nor shall I readily forget a certain house in
the Quadrant where a visitor died, and a
dark old woman continued to dwell alone
with the dead body ; nor how this old woman
conceived a hatred to myself and one of my
cousins, and in the dread hour of the dusk,
as we were clambering on the garden-walls,
opened a window in that house of mortality
and cursed us in a shrill voice and with a
marrowy choice of language. It was a pair
of very colourless urchins that fled down the
lane from this remarkable experience ! But
I recall with a more doubtful sentiment,
compounded out of fear and exultation, the
coil of equinoctial tempests ; trumpeting
squalls, scouring flaws of rain ; the boats
with their reefed lugsails scudding for
the harbour mouth, where danger lay, for
it was hard to make when the wind had
any east in it ; the wives clustered with
blowing shawls at the pier-head, where (if
fate was against them) they might see boat
and husband and sons—their whole wealth
and their whole family—engulfed under their
eyes ; and (what I saw but once) a troop
of neighbours forcing such an unfortunate
homeward, and she squalling and battling in
their midst, a figure scarcely human, a tragic
Mænad.

THE LANTERN BEARERS

These are things that I recall with interest ; but what my memory dwells upon the most, I have been all this while withholding. It was a sport peculiar to the place, and indeed to a week or so of our two months' holiday there. Maybe it still flourishes in its native spot ; for boys and their pastimes are swayed by periodic forces inscrutable to man ; so that tops and marbles reappear in their due season, regular like the sun and moon ; and the harmless art of knuckle-bones has seen the fall of the Roman empire and the rise of the United States. It may still flourish in its native spot, but nowhere else, I am persuaded ; for I tried myself to introduce it on Tweedside, and was defeated lamentably ; its charm being quite local, like a country wine that cannot be exported.

The idle manner of it was this :—

Toward the end of September, when school-time was drawing near and the nights were already black, we would begin to sally from our respective villas, each equipped with a tin bull's-eye lantern. The thing was so well known that it had worn a rut in the commerce of Great Britain ; and the grocers, about the due time, began to garnish their windows with our particular brand of luminary. We wore them buckled to the waist upon a cricket belt, and over them, such was the rigour of the game, a buttoned top-coat. They smelled noisomely of blistered tin ; they never burned aright, though they would always burn our fingers ; their use was naught ; the pleasure of them merely fanciful ; and yet a boy with a bull's-eye under his top-coat asked for nothing more. The fishermen used lanterns about their boats, and it was from them, I suppose, that we got the hint ; but theirs were not bull's-eyes, nor did we ever play at being fishermen. The police carried them at their belts, and we had plainly copied them in that ; yet we did not pretend to be policemen. Burglars, indeed, we may have had some haunting thoughts of ; and we had certainly an eye to past ages when lanterns were more common, and to certain story-books in which we had found them to figure very largely. But take it for all in all, the pleasure of the thing was substantive ; and to be a boy with a bull's-eye under his top-coat was good enough for us.

When two of these asses met, there would be an anxious " Have you got your lantern ? " and a gratified " Yes ! " That was the shibboleth, and very needful too ; for, as it was the rule to keep our glory contained, none could recognise a lantern-bearer, unless (like the polecat) by the smell. Four or five would sometimes climb into the belly of a ten-man lugger, with nothing but the thwarts above them—for the cabin was usually locked, or choose out some hollow of the links where the wind might whistle overhead. There the coats would be unbuttoned and the bull's-eyes discovered; and in the chequering glimmer, under the huge windy hall of the night, and cheered by a rich steam of toasting tinware, these fortunate young gentlemen would crouch together in the cold sand of the links or on the scaly bilges of the fishing-boat, and delight themselves with inappropriate talk. Woe is me that I may not give some specimens—some of their foresights of life, or deep inquiries into the rudiments of man and nature, these were so fiery and so innocent, they were so richly silly, so romantically young. But the talk, at any rate, was but a condiment; and these gatherings themselves only accidents in the career of the lantern-bearer. The essence of this bliss was to walk by yourself in the black night; the slide shut, the top-coat buttoned; not a ray escaping, whether to conduct your footsteps or to make your glory public: a mere pillar of darkness in the dark; and all the while, deep down in the privacy of your fool's heart, to know you had a bull's-eye at your belt, and to exult and sing over the knowledge.

ROBERT LOUIS STEVENSON

II

It is said that a poet has died young in the breast of the most stolid. It may be contended, rather, that this (somewhat minor) bard in almost every case survives, and is the spice of life to his possessor. Justice is not done to the versatility and the unplumbed childishness of man's imagination. His life from without may seem but a rude mound of mud ; there will be some golden chamber at the heart of it, in which he dwells delighted ; and for as dark as his pathway seems to the observer, he will have some kind of a bull's-eye at his belt.

It would be hard to pick out a career more cheerless than that of Dancer, the miser, as he figures in the " Old Bailey Reports," a prey to the most sordid persecutions, the butt of his neighbourhood, betrayed by his hired man, his house beleagured by the impish schoolboy, and he himself grinding and fuming and impotently fleeing to the law against these pinpricks. You marvel at first that any one should willingly prolong a life so destitute of charm and dignity ; and then you call to memory that had he chosen, had he ceased to be a miser, he could have been freed at once from these trials, and might have built himself a castle and gone escorted by a squadron.

For the love of more recondite joys, which we
cannot estimate, which, it may be, we should
envy, the man had willingly forgone both
comfort and consideration. " His mind to
him a kingdom was " ; and sure enough,
digging into that mind, which seems at first
a dust-heap, we unearth some priceless jewels.
For Dancer must have had the love of
power and the disdain of using it, a noble
character in itself ; disdain of many pleasures,
a chief part of which is commonly called
wisdom ; disdain of the inevitable end, that
finest trait of mankind ; scorn of men's
opinions, another element of virtue ; and at
the back of all, a conscience just like yours
and mine, whining like a cur, swindling like a
thimble-rigger, but still pointing (there or
thereabout) to some conventional standard.
Here were a cabinet portrait to which Hawthorne perhaps had done justice ; and yet
not Hawthorne either, for he was mildly
minded, and it lay not in him to create for us
that throb of the miser's pulse, his fretful
energy of gusto, his vast arms of ambition
clutching in he knows not what : insatiable,
insane, a god with a muck-rake. Thus, at
least, looking in the bosom of the miser, consideration detects the poet in the full tide of
life, with more, indeed, of the poetic fire than
usually goes to epics ; and tracing that mean

man about his cold hearth, and to and fro in his discomfortable house, spies within him a blazing bonfire of delight. And so with others, who do not live by bread alone, but by some cherished and perhaps fantastic pleasure ; who are meat salesmen to the external eye, and possibly to themselves are Shakespeares, Napoleons, or Beethovens ; who have not one virtue to rub against another in the field of active life, and yet perhaps, in the life of contemplation, sit with the saints. We see them on the street, and we can count their buttons ; but heaven knows in what they pride themselves ! heaven knows where they have set their treasure !

There is one fable that touches very near the quick of life ; the fable of the monk who passed into the woods, heard a bird break into song, hearkened for a trill or two, and found himself on his return a stranger at his convent gates ; for he had been absent fifty years, and of all his comrades there survived but one to recognise him. It is not only in the woods that this enchanter carols, though perhaps he is native there. He sings in the most doleful places. The miser hears him and chuckles, and the days are moments. With no more apparatus than an ill-smelling lantern I have evoked him on the naked links. All life that is not merely mechanical is spun out of two strands : seeking for that bird and hearing him. And it is just this that makes life so hard to value, and the delight of each so incommunicable. And just a knowledge of this, and a remembrance of those fortunate hours in which the bird has sung to us, that fills us with such wonder when we turn the pages of the realist. There, to be sure, we find a picture of life in so far as it consists of mud and old iron, cheap desires and cheap fears, that which we are ashamed to remember, and that which we are careless whether we forget ; but of the note of that time-devouring nightingale we hear no news.

The case of these writers of romance is most obscure. They have been boys and youths ; they have lingered outside the window of the beloved, who was then most probably writing to someone else ; they have sat before a sheet of paper, and felt themselves mere continents of congested poetry, not one line of which would flow ; they have walked alone in the woods, they have walked in cities under the countless lamps ; they have been to sea, they have hated, they have feared, they have longed to knife a man, and maybe done it ; the wild taste of life has stung their palate. Or, if you deny them all the rest, one pleasure at least they have tasted to the full—their books are there to prove it—the keen pleasure

of successful literary compositions. And yet
they fill the globe with volumes, whose clever-
ness inspires me with despairing admiration,
and whose consistent falsity to all I care to
call existence, with despairing wrath. If I
had no better hope than to continue to revolve
among the dreary and petty businesses, and
to be moved by the paltry hopes and fears
with which they surround and animate their
heroes, I declare I would die now. But there
has never an hour of mine gone quite so dully
yet; if it were spent waiting at a railway
junction, I would have some scattering thoughts,
I could count some grains of memory, compared to which the whole of one of these
romances seems but dross.

These writers would retort (if I take them
properly) that this was very true; that it
was the same with themselves and other
persons of (what they call) the artistic temperament; that in this we were exceptional,
and should apparently be ashamed of ourselves; but that our works must deal exclusively with (what they call) the average man,
who was a prodigious dull fellow, and quite
dead to all but the paltriest considerations.
I accept the issue. We can only know others
by ourselves. The artistic temperament (a
plague on the expression!) does not make us
different from our fellow-men, or it would

make us incapable of writing novels ; and
the average man (a murrain on the word !)
is just like you and me, or he would not be
average. It was Whitman who stamped a
kind of Birmingham sacredness upon the
latter phrase ; but Whitman knew very well,
and showed very nobly, that the average man
was full of joys and full of a poetry of his own.
And this harping on life's dullness and man's
meanness is a loud profession of incompetence ;
it is one of two things : the cry of the blind
eye, *I cannot see,* or the complaint of the
dumb tongue, *I cannot utter.* To draw a life
without delights is to prove I have not realised
it. To picture a man without some sort of
poetry—well, it goes near to prove my case,
for it shows an author may have little enough.
To see Dancer only as a dirty, old, small-
minded, impotently fuming man, in a dirty
house, besieged by Harrow boys, and probably
beset by small attorneys, is to show myself
as keen an observer as . . . the Harrow boys.
But these young gentlemen (with a more be-
coming modesty) were content to pluck Dancer
by the coat-tails ; they did not suppose they
had surprised his secret or could put him living
in a book : and it is there my error would
have lain. Or say that in the same romance—
I continue to call these books romances, in
the hope of giving pain—say that in the same

romance, which now begins really to take
shape, I should leave to speak of Dancer, and
follow instead the Harrow boys; and say
that I came on some such business as that of
my lantern-bearers on the links; and described
the boys as very cold, spat upon by flurries of
rain, and drearily surrounded, all of which
they were; and their talk as silly and indecent,
which it certainly was. I might upon these
lines, and had I Zola's genius, turn out, in a
page or so, a gem of literary art, render the
lantern-light with the touches of a master,
and lay on the indecency with the ungrudging
hand of love; and when all was done, what
a triumph would my picture be of shallowness
and dullness! how it would have missed the
point! how it would have belied the boys!
To the ear of the stenographer, the talk is
merely silly and indecent; but ask the boys
themselves, and they are discussing (as it is
highly proper they should) the possibilities of
existence. To the eye of the observer they
are wet and cold, and drearily surrounded;
but ask themselves, and they are in the heaven
of a recondite pleasure, the ground of which
is an ill-smelling lantern.

III

For, to repeat, the ground of a man's joy is
often hard to hit. It may hinge at times

upon a mere accessory, like the lantern; it may reside, like Dancer's, in the mysterious inwards of psychology. It may consist with perpetual failure, and find exercise in the continued chase. It has so little bond with externals (such as the observer scribbles in his note-book) that it may even touch them not; and the man's true life, for which he consents to live, lie altogether in the field of fancy. The clergyman, in his spare hours, may be winning battles, the farmer sailing ships, the banker reaping triumph in the arts: all leading another life, plying another trade from that they chose; like the poet's housebuilder, who, after all, is cased in stone,

" By his fireside, as impotent fancy prompts.
Rebuilds it to his liking."

In such a case the poetry runs underground. The observer (poor soul, with his documents!) is all abroad. For to look at the man is but to court deception. We shall see the trunk from which he draws his nourishment; but he himself is above and abroad in the green dome of foliage, hummed through by winds and nested in by nightingales. And the true realism were that of the poets, to climb up after him like a squirrel, and catch some glimpse of the heaven for which he lives. And the true realism, always and everywhere, is

that of the poets: to find out where joy
resides, and give it a voice far beyond singing.

For to miss the joy is to miss all. In the
joy of the actors lies the sense of any action.
That is the explanation, that the excuse. To
one who has not the secret of the lanterns,
the scene upon the links is meaningless. And
hence the haunting and truly spectral un-
reality of realistic books. Hence, when we
read the English realists, the incredulous
wonder with which we observe the hero's
constancy under the submerging tide of dullness, and how he bears up with his jibbing
sweetheart, and endures the chatter of idiot
girls, and stands by his whole unfeatured
wilderness of an existence, instead of seeking
relief in drink or foreign travel. Hence in
the French, in that meat-market of middle-
aged sensuality, the disgusted surprise with
which we see the hero drift sidelong, and
practically quite untempted, into every description of misconduct and dishonour. In
each, we miss the personal poetry, the enchanted
atmosphere, that rainbow work of fancy that
clothes what is naked and seems to ennoble
what is base; in each, life falls dead like
dough, instead of soaring away like a balloon
into the colours of the sunset; each is true,
each inconceivable; for no man lives in the
external truth, among salts and acids, but in

the warm, phantasmagoric chamber of his brain, with the painted windows and the storied walls.

Of this falsity we have had a recent example from a man who knows far better— Tolstoi's *Powers of Darkness*. Here is a piece full of force and truth, yet quite untrue. For before Mikita was led into so dire a situation he was tempted, and temptations are beautiful at least in part ; and the work which dwells on the ugliness of crime and gives no hint of any loveliness in the temptation, sins against the modesty of life, and even when a Tolstoi writes it, sinks to melodrama. The peasants are not understood ; they saw their life in fairer colours ; even the deaf girl was clothed in poetry for Mikita, or he had never fallen. And so, once again, even an Old Bailey melodrama, without some brightness of poetry and lustre of existence, falls into the inconceivable and ranks with fairy tales.

IV

In nobler books we are moved with something like the emotions of life ; and this emotion is very variously provoked. We are so moved when Levine labours in the field, when André sinks beyond emotion, when Richard Feveral and Lucy Desborough meet beside the river, when Antony, " not cowardly, puts off his helmet," when Kent has infinite pity on the dying Lear, when, in Dostoieffsky's *Despised and Rejected,* the uncomplaining hero drains his cup of suffering and virtue. These are notes that please the great heart of man. Not only love, and the fields, and the bright face of danger, but sacrifice and death and unmerited suffering humbly supported, touch in us the vein of the poetic. We love to think of them, we long to try them, we are humbly hopeful that we may prove heroes also.

We have heard, perhaps, too much of lesser matters. Here is the door, here is the open air. *Itur in antiquam silvam.*

E. V. LUCAS

[1868———]

" MY COUSIN, THE BOOKBINDER " *

*" Oh, I am so poorly ! I waked it at my cousin's, the bookbinder, who is now with God."—*CHARLES LAMB, *to P. G. Patmore, 1827.*

"SO you've been reading that, sir, have you : I have a copy too. I'll fetch it and show you. . . . The inscription ? Oh, yes that's all right. He's my cousin, true enough : his real name's not Elia, of course ; his real name's Lamb— Charles Lamb. He's a clerk at the East India Company's in Leadenhall Street—a little dark man with a large head. Must be nearly fifty by this time.

" ' Genius,' you say ? Well, I've heard others say that too—one or two persons, that is : customers of mine ; but I don't know. Perhaps I'm no judge of such things. I'm a bookbinder. The outside of books is my line, not the inside. Oh yes, I've read Elia's

* From " Character and Comedy " (Methuen).

E. V. LUCAS

Essays—not all through, perhaps, but here and there. Quite enough to tell, anyway.

" ' Genius,' you say ? My idea of genius is not that. I like a straightforward thing. Did you ever read the *Elegy in a Country Church-yard*, by Thomas Gray ? Now, there's genius. So beautifully it goes—never a trip to the tongue from beginning to end, and everything so clear a child could understand it, and yet it's literature too. My little girl used to say it. *Rasselas*, too —do you know that ? The Happy Valley and all the rest of it. That's genius,.I think. But not this twisted stuff going backwards and forwards and one never feeling quite sure how to take it. I like a plain man with a plain mind.

" It's just the same with my cousin when you meet him. You never know what he's at. He's so nice sometimes, all heart, and friendly—and then the next time I have a notion that every-thing he says means something else. He leads me on to talk—just as I am talking now to you, sir,—and he seems to agree with what I say so warmly ; and then all of a sudden I see that he's just making fun of me all the time. He must have his joke. He comes in here some-times on his way from the office, and precious little he does there, I can tell you. Oh, they're an easy lot, those East India clerks.

" But with all his odd ways and that mis-chievous mouth of his, his heart's in the right

place. Very different from his brother, who
died a year or so back. He was nothing to
boast of; but the airs that man used to put
on! I remember his father well—a little
brisk man, wonderfully like Garrick, full of
jokes and bright, quick ways. He was really
a scrivener, but he didn't do much of that in
those days, having fallen into an easy place
with old Mr. Salt, the Member of Parliament,
and a great man in the law. This Mr. Salt
lived in the Temple, and little John Lamb—
that is your Elia's father—he was his servant :
did everything for him and lived in clover.
Mrs. Lamb, she cooked. Mr. Salt was the
generous kind—sent the boys to school and
all the rest of it. They had it all their own
way till the old gentleman died, and then
things went wrong one after the other. It's
too sad to talk about. . . .

" Except that Mrs. Lamb and her husband's
sister, Miss Sarah—' Aunt Hetty ' they used
to call her—never quite hit it off, it was as
happy a family as you'd ask for. But there
came terrible times. . . . It's too sad. . . .
Where was I ?—Oh yes, so you see that Mr.
John Lamb, Esquire, who died the other day,
had little enough to boast of, but he walked
about as if he owned the earth. He used to
come in here now and then to give me an order,
and he threw it to me as if it was a bone and

I was a dog. Many's the time I had it on my
tongue to remind him what his father was,
but I kept it back. A word unsaid is still to
say. He was at the South Sea House, near his
brother in Leadenhall Street, but they didn't
have much to do with each other. Mr. John,
he was a big blustering, happy man, while this
little one who calls himself Elia is all for
quietness and not being seen, and having his
own thoughts and his own jokes. They hadn't
much in common. . . .

" Besides, there was another thing. There's
a sister, you must know, sir, a wonderful wise
woman, but she's not always quite right in her
head, poor dear ; and when it was a question
of whether someone had to promise to be re-
sponsible for her, or she must go into an asylum
for the rest of her life, her younger brother,
the writer of that book there, under your arm,
said *he* would ; and he gave up everything,
and has kept her—it was thirty years ago very
nearly—ever since. Well, it was thought in
the family and by their friends that John, who
was a grown man at the time, and a bachelor
too, and beginning to be prosperous, ought to
have done more than he did, and I think that
sometimes he thought so too, although he was
usually pretty well satisfied with himself.
Anyway, he didn't go to see his brother and
sister much, and when he did I've heard that

there was often trouble, because he would have
his own way and argufy until he lost his temper.
I was told as how he once had a dispute with
Mr. Hazlitt the writer over something to do
with painting, and knocked him down. Just
think of knocking a man down about a matter
of paint ! But your high-handed men will
quarrel over anything.

" Like his little brother he tried writing too,
but he couldn't do it. He wrote a little tract
on kindness to animals, and brought it here to
be bound in morocco. Not to give away,
mind, but to keep. ' Author's Copy ' I had
to letter it. . . . ' Kindness to animals,' I
nearly said to him ; ' what about kindness to
sisters ? ' But I didn't say it.

" The sister ? Ah, yes, she's the pick.
She's a great woman, if ever there was one.
I know her better than any of them, because
when they were living near here, and her
brother—your Mr. Lamb, the author—was at
his office, I often looked in with a pork chop
or some little thing like that. There's no
jokes about her ; no saying things that she
doesn't mean, or anything like that. She's
all gold, my cousin Mary is. She understands
everything, too. I've taken lots of troubles
to her—little difficulties about my children,
and what not—and she understands directly,
for all she's an old maid, and tells me just

what I want to know. She's the clever one.
She can write too. I've got a little book of her
stories and some poetry for children—here they
are—I bound them myself : that's the best
binding I can do—real russia, and hand tooling,
every bit of it. Did she write all of them ?
No, she didn't write all, but she wrote the best.
Her brother Charles did something to each, but
I don't mind that. I think of them as her
books, Mary's. If only she had better health,
she would write much better than he does ;
but her poor head. . . . Every year, you must
know, she goes out of her mind for a little
while. Oh, it's too sad. . . .

"Have they many friends ? Oh yes, a
good many. Most of them are too clever for
me ; but there are some old-fashioned ones
too, that they like for old sakes' sake. They're
the best. One or two of them are very good
customers of mine. There's Mr. Robinson, the
barrister, he brings me lots of books to mend,
and I've had work for Mr. Aders, too. But
as for your Mr. Lamb,—Elia,—never a stitch
will he let you put into any book, even if it's
dropping to pieces. Why, he won't even take
the dealer's tickets off them. He never
thinks of the outside of a book, but you
should see him tearing the heart out of them
by the light of one candle. I'm told he knows
more about what books are worth reading than

anyone living. That's odd, isn't it, and his
father a little serving-man ! Life's full of
surprises. They say he knows all about poetry,
too, and helped the great poets. There's Mr.
Wordsworth, why, he dedicated a book to my
cousin,—I've got it here, *The Waggoner*, a
pretty book it is, too,—and Mr. Coleridge, who
wrote about the old sailor man and the alba-
tross, he let my cousin put some little poems
of his own into one of his books. It turns one
inside out when one thinks of this, and then
of the old days and his father powdering Mr.
Salt's wig. But I suppose everyone's father
had to work once. Still, it's funnier when one
belongs to the same family.

" Now I come to remember it, his father used
to write a little too—free and easy pieces for a
charitable society he belonged to, and so on.
It's odd how writing runs in a family. But there
won't be any more Lambs to write—John left
no children, only a stepdaughter, and Charles and
Mary are single. This is the end. Well . . .

" Yes, they've moved from London now.
They're living in Islington. They used to live
in the Temple for years, and then they went
to Covent Garden, over a tinman's. Miss
Lamb liked that better than the Temple, but
her brother liked the Temple best. It gave
her more to do, poor dear, during the day,
because her sitting-room window looked over

Bow Street, and she could see all that was going on. I'm afraid Islington is very dull after that. She could see the two great theatres, too, and they both love the play.

"He wrote a farce once. I went to see it. Nearly twenty years ago, at the Lane, when Elliston had it. We had orders for the pit, my wife and I, and the house was full of clerks from the South Sea House and the East India House. But it wouldn't do. *Mr. H.* it was called, and the whole joke was about the man's full name. But it wouldn't do. No one really minds names, and his wasn't so monstrously bad—only Hogsflesh, when all was said and done. All the friends did what we could for it, and the gentlemen from the great offices cheered and clapped, but the Noes got it. I never heard such hissing. I climbed up on the seat to see how poor Miss Lamb and her brother were taking it,—they were right in front, just by the orchestra,— and there was he, hissing away louder than anyone. Think of it, hissing his own play! It's one of the best jokes I ever heard. But she, poor dear, she was just crying.

"No, he never tried the stage again, not to my knowledge. But I always say it wasn't a bad little play. If he'd only have let his sister touch it up, it would have been all right.

" MY COUSIN, THE BOOKBINDER "

She would have told him that Hogsflesh wasn't a good enough joke.   She knows. . . .

" I went up to Islington to see them only last week, but he was out.   A nice little cottage, but very quiet for her.   Nothing to see but the houses over the way, and the New River, and the boys fishing for sticklebacks all day long. The river's absolutely in front of the house : nothing between you and it.   Have you ever heard of Mr. Dyer, the writer ?   An old man, nearly blind.   Well, he was coming away from my cousin's one day last year, and he walked bang into the water before anyone could stop him.   Plump in.   It's a wonder he wasn't drowned.   There was an account of it in the *London Magazine* for December ;   for my cousin's a terrible man to serve up his friends and have jokes against them.   He writes about everything just as it happens.   I'm always expecting he'll have me in one of his essays. In fact, to tell you a secret, sir, that's why I read them.   But I don't think he's got me yet.

" Yes, Islington's very different from Covent Garden, and the Temple too ;   for though the Temple is quiet enough, you've only got to pop into Fleet Street to be in the thick of everything.   When they lived there she used to like doing her shopping in Fetter Lane, because it was at the top of the lane that she used to go to school years and years ago.   For

she's getting to be an old woman, you know.
Let me see, how old is she?—Why, let's see,
when was Mary born? It must have been 1763;
no, it was 1764. Why, she'll be sixty this year.

"What does she do all day? Well, she
reads a great deal, stories for the most part.
And she sews. She's very good with her
needle. And then she has her thoughts. And
at night they play cards. He gets back pretty
soon, you know. Those East India gentlemen
they don't do too much, I can tell you, and
I'm told he's one of the laziest. Always either
talking or writing letters, I hear. There's a
good story of him down there. One of the
superiors met him coming in at about half-
past ten, and he said to him, sharp-like,
'Mr. Lamb,' he said, 'you come very late.'
And what do you think my cousin said, the
impudent little fellow? 'Yes,' he said, as
cool as you like, 'yes,' he said, 'but see how
early I go,' he said. I can't say it as he did,
because he stammers and stutters and I'm no
mimic: but the brass of it shut the gentleman
up. My cousin told me himself. He likes to
tell you his good things; but I can't understand
a lot of them. Everyone has a different idea
of what's funny. I'm with him, though,
about old Munden: I could laugh at him
all night.

"I'm troubled about them up there, so far

from London and the theatres and the noise.
It's a mistake to give up so much all at once.
And they've given up their regular evenings,
too, when people came in to play cards and talk.
You can't ask busy folk to go to Islington.

" My cousin told me some bad news last
week. She says that your Mr. Lamb,—Elia,—
although he has such an easy time and a large
salary, wants to leave the East India House
and do nothing. I hope they won't let him.
I know enough of life and of him to see what
a mistake it would be. It was a mistake to go
to Islington: it will be a worse mistake to retire.
He says he wants to live in the country; but
he doesn't really. Authors don't know what
they want. I always say that every author
ought to have a bookbinder to advise him.

" She knows it's all wrong, poor dear, but
what can she do ? He worries so. She sees
him all miserable, and after she's said all she
can against his plans, she agrees with them.
That's like good women. When they see that
what must be must be, they do their best.
But it is very sad. . . . It's her I'm so sorry
for. He's the kind of man that ought to go
to business every day.

" Well, sir, good night to you. I hope I
haven't been tedious with all my talk.

" No, sir, not quite a genius ; but very
clever, I grant you."

HILAIRE BELLOC

[1870———]

THE MOWING OF A FIELD*

THERE is a valley in South England remote from ambition and from fear, where the passage of strangers is rare and unperceived, and where the scent of the grass in summer is breathed only by those who are native to that unvisited land. The roads to the Channel do not traverse it ; they choose upon either side easier passes over the range. One track alone leads up through it to the hills, and this is changeable : now green, where men have little occasion to go, now a good road where it nears the homesteads and the barns. The woods grow steep above the slopes ; they reach sometimes the very summit of the heights, or, when they cannot attain them, fill in and clothe the coombes. And, in between, along the floor of the valley, deep pastures and their silence are bordered by lawns of chalky grass and the small yew trees of the Downs.

* From " Hills and the Sea " (Methuen).

THE MOWING OF A FIELD

The clouds that visit its sky reveal themselves beyond the one great rise, and sail, white and enormous, to the other, and sink beyond that other. But the plains above which they have travelled and the Weald to which they go, the people of the valley cannot see and hardly recall. The wind, when it reaches such fields, is no longer a gale from the salt, but fruitful and soft, an inland breeze; and those whose blood was nourished here feel in that wind the fruitfulness of our orchards and all the life that all things draw from the air.

In this place, when I was a boy, I pushed through a fringe of beeches that made a complete screen between me and the world, and I came to a glade called No Man's Land. I climbed beyond it, and I was surprised and glad, because from the ridge of that glade I saw the sea. To this place very lately I returned.

The many things that I recovered as I came up the countryside were not less charming than when a distant memory had enshrined them, but much more. Whatever veil is thrown by a longing recollection had not intensified nor even made more mysterious the beauty of that happy ground; not in my very dreams of morning had I, in exile, seen it more beloved or more rare. Much also that I had forgotten now returned to me as I

approached—a group of elms, a little turn of
the parson's wall, a small paddock beyond the
graveyard close, cherished by one man, with
a low wall of very old stone guarding it all
round. And all these things fulfilled and
amplified my delight, till even the good vision
of the place, which I had kept so many years,
left me and was replaced by its better reality.
" Here," I said to myself, " is a symbol of
what some say is reserved for the soul : pleasure
of a kind which cannot be imagined save in a
moment when at last it is attained."

When I came to my own gate and my own
field, and had now before me the house I knew,
I looked round a little (though it was already
evening), and I saw that the grass was standing
as it should stand when it is ready for the
scythe. For in this, as in everything that a
man can do—of those things at least which
are very old—there is an exact moment when
they are done best. And it has been remarked
of whatever rules us that it works blunderingly,
seeing that the good things given to a man
are not given at the precise moment when
they would have filled him with delight. But,
whether this be true or false, we can choose
the just turn of the seasons in everything we
do of our own will, and especially in the
making of hay. Many think that hay is best
made when the grass is thickest ; and so they

delay until it is rank and in flower, and has already heavily pulled the ground. And there is another false reason for delay, which is wet weather. For very few will understand (though it comes year after year) that we have rain always in South England between the sickle and the scythe, or say just after the weeks of east wind are over. First we have a week of sudden warmth, as though the south had come to see us all ; then we have the weeks of east and south-east wind ; and then we have more or less of that rain of which I spoke, and which always astonishes the world. Now it is just before, or during, or at the very end of that rain—but not later—that grass should be cut for hay. True, upland grass, which is always thin, should be cut earlier than the grass in the bottoms and along the water meadows ; but not even the latest, even in the wettest seasons, should be left, as it is, to flower and even to seed. For what we get when we store our grass is not a harvest of something ripe, but a thing just caught in its prime before maturity : as witness that our corn and straw are best yellow, but our hay is best green. So also Death should be represented with a scythe and Time with a sickle; for Time can take only what is ripe, but Death comes always too soon. In a word, then, it is always much easier to cut grass too late than

HILAIRE BELLOC

too early; and I, under that evening and come back to these pleasant fields, looked at the grass and knew that it was time. June was in full advance: it was the beginning of that season when the night has already lost her foothold of the earth and hovers over it, never quite descending, but mixing sunset with the dawn.

Next morning, before it was yet broad day, I awoke, and thought of the mowing. The birds were already chattering in the trees beside my window, all except the nightingale, which had left and flown away to the Weald, where he sings all summer by day as well as by night in the oaks and the hazel spinneys, and especially along the little river Adur, one of the rivers of the Weald. The birds and the thought of the mowing had awakened me, and I went down the stairs and along the stone floors to where I could find a scythe; and when I took it from its nail, I remembered how, fourteen years ago, I had last gone out with my scythe, just so, into the fields at morning. In between that day and this were many things, cities and armies, and a confusion of books, mountains and the desert, and horrible great breadths of sea.

When I got out into the long grass the sun was not yet risen, but there were already many colours in the eastern sky, and I made haste

280

to sharpen my scythe, so that I might get to the cutting before the dew should dry. Some say that it is best to wait till all the dew has risen, so as to get the grass quite dry from the very first. But, though it is an advantage to get the grass quite dry, yet it is not worth while to wait till the dew has risen. For, in the first place, you lose many hours of work (and those the coolest), and next—which is more important—you lose that great ease and thickness in cutting which comes of the dew. So I at once began to sharpen my scythe.

There is an art also in the sharpening of a scythe, and it is worth describing carefully. Your blade must be dry, and that is why you will see men rubbing the scythe-blade with grass before they whet it. Then also your rubber must be quite dry, and on this account it is a good thing to lay it on your coat and keep it there during all your day's mowing. The scythe you stand upright, with the blade pointing away from you, and you put your left hand firmly on the back of the blade, grasping it; then you pass the rubber first down one side of the blade-edge and then down the other, beginning near the handle and going on to the point and working quickly and hard. When you first do this you will, perhaps, cut your hand; but it is only at first that such an accident will happen to you.

281

To tell when the scythe is sharp enough this is the rule. First the stone clangs and grinds against the iron harshly ; then it rings musically to one note ; then, at last, it purrs as though the iron and stone were exactly suited. When you hear this, your scythe is sharp enough ; and I, when I heard it that June dawn, with everything quite silent except the birds, let down the scythe and bent myself to mow.

When one does anything anew, after so many years, one fears very much for one's trick or habit. But all things once learnt are easily recoverable, and I very soon recovered the swing and power of the mower. Mowing well and mowing badly—or rather, not mowing at all—are separated by very little ; as is also true of writing verse, of playing the fiddle, and of dozens of other things, but of nothing more than of believing. For the bad or young or untaught mower without tradition, the mower Promethean, the mower original and contemptuous of the past, does all these things. He leaves great crescents of grass uncut. He digs the point of the scythe hard into the ground with a jerk. He loosens the handles and even the fastening of the blade. He twists the blade with his blunders, he blunts the blade, he chips it, dulls it, or breaks it clean off at the tip. If

any one is standing by he cuts him in the
ankle. He sweeps up into the air wildly,
with nothing to resist his stroke. He drags
up earth with the grass, which is like making
the meadow bleed. But the good mower who
does things just as they should be done and
have been for a hundred thousand years, falls
into none of these fooleries. He goes forward
very steadily, his scythe-blade just barely
missing the ground, every grass falling; the
swish and rhythm of his mowing are always
the same.

So great an art can only be learnt by continual practice; but this much is worth
writing down, that, as in all good work, to
know the thing with which you work is the
core of the affair. Good verse is best written
on good paper with an easy pen, not with a
lump of coal on a whitewashed wall. The
pen thinks for you; and so does the scythe
mow for you if you treat it honourably and
in a manner that makes it recognise its service.
The manner is this. You must regard the
scythe as a pendulum that swings, not as a
knife that cuts. A good mower puts no more
strength into his stroke than into his lifting.
Again, stand up to your work. The bad
mower, eager and full of pain, leans forward
and tries to force the scythe through the grass.
The good mower, serene and able, stands as

nearly straight as the shape of the scythe will
let him, and follows up every stroke closely,
moving his left foot forward. Then also let
every stroke get well away. Mowing is a
thing of ample gestures, like drawing a cartoon.
Then, again, get yourself into a mechanical
and repetitive mood : be thinking of anything
at all but your mowing, and be anxious only
when there seems some interruption to the
monotony of the sound. In this mowing
should be like one's prayers—all of a sort and
always the same, and so made that you can
establish a monotony and work them, as it
were, with half your mind : that happier half,
the half that does not bother.

In this way, when I had recovered the art
after so many years, I went forward over
the field, cutting lane after lane through the
grass, and bringing out its most secret essences
with the sweep of the scythe until the air was
full of odours. At the end of every lane I
sharpened my scythe and looked back at the
work done, and then carried my scythe down
again upon my shoulder to begin another.
So, long before the bell rang in the chapel
above me—that is, long before six o'clock,
which is the time for the *Angelus*—I had
many swathes already lying in order parallel
like soldiery ; and the high grass yet standing,
making a great contrast with the shaven part,

looked dense and high. As it says in the
Ballad of Val-ès-Dunes, where—

> "The tall son of the Seven Winds
> Came riding out of Hither-hythe,"

and his horse-hoofs (you will remember)
trampled into the press and made a gap in
it, and his sword (as you know)—

> " . . . was like a scythe
> In Arcus when the grass is high
> And all the swathes in order lie,
> And there's the bailiff standing by
> A-gathering of the tithe."

So I mowed all that morning, till the houses
awoke in the valley, and from some of them
rose a little fragrant smoke, and men began
to be seen.

I stood still and rested on my scythe to
watch the awakening of the village, when
I saw coming up to my field a man whom I
had known in older times, before I had left
the Valley.

He was of that dark, silent race upon which
all the learned quarrel, but which, by whatever meaningless name it may be called—
Iberian, or Celtic, or what you will—is the
permanent root of all England, and makes
England wealthy and preserves it everywhere,
except perhaps in the Fens and in a part of
Yorkshire. Everywhere else you will find it

active and strong. These people are intensive;
their thoughts and their labours turn inward.
It is on account of their presence in these
islands that our gardens are the richest in the
world. They also love low rooms and ample
fires and great warm slopes of thatch. They
have, as I believe, an older acquaintance with
the English air than any other of all the
strains that make up England. They hunted
in the Weald with stones, and camped in the
pines of the green-sand. They lurked under
the oaks of the upper rivers, and saw the
legionaries go up, up the straight, paved
road from the sea. They helped the few
pirates to destroy the towns, and mixed with
those pirates and shared the spoils of the
Roman villas, and were glad to see the cap-
tains and the priests destroyed. They remain;
and no admixture of the Frisian pirates, or
the Breton, or the Angevin and Norman
conquerors, has very much affected their
cunning eyes.

To this race, I say, belonged the man who
now approached me. And he said to me,
" Mowing ? " And I answered, " Ar." Then
he also said, " Ar," as in duty bound; for so
we speak to each other in the Stenes of the
Downs.

Next he told me that, as he had nothing to
do, he would lend me a hand; and I thanked

him warmly, or, as we say, "kindly." For
it is a good custom of ours always to treat
bargaining as though it were a courteous
pastime; and though what he was after was
money, and what I wanted was his labour at
the least pay, yet we both played the comedy
that we were free men, the one granting a
grace and the other accepting it. For the
dry bones of commerce, avarice and method
and need, are odious to the Valley; and we
cover them up with a pretty body of fiction
and observances. Thus, when it comes to
buying pigs, the buyer does not begin to
decry the pig and the vendor to praise it, as
is the custom with lesser men; but tradition
makes them do business in this fashion :—

First the buyer will go up to the seller when
he sees him in his own steading, and, looking
at the pig with admiration, the buyer will say
that rain may or may not fall, or that we shall
have snow or thunder, according to the time
of year. Then the seller, looking critically at
the pig, will agree that the weather is as his
friend maintains. There is no haste at all;
great leisure marks the dignity of their exchange. And the next step is, that the buyer
says: "That's a fine pig you have there,
Mr. —— " (giving the seller's name). "Ar,
powerful fine pig." Then the seller, saying
also "Mr." (for twin brothers rocked in one

287

cradle give each other ceremonious observance here), the seller, I say, admits, as though with reluctance, the strength and beauty of the pig, and falls into deep thought. Then the buyer says, as though moved by a great desire, that he is ready to give so much for the pig, naming half the proper price, or a little less. Then the seller remains in silence for some moments ; and at last begins to shake his head slowly, till he says : " I don't be thinking of selling the pig, anyways." He will also add that a party only Wednesday offered him so much for the pig—and he names about double the proper price. Thus all ritual is duly accomplished ; and the solemn act is entered upon with reverence and in a spirit of truth. For when the buyer uses this phrase : " I'll tell you what I *will* do," and offers within half a crown of the pig's value, the seller replies that he can refuse him nothing, and names half a crown above its value ; the difference is split, the pig is sold, and in the quiet soul of each runs the peace of something accomplished.

Thus do we buy a pig or land or labour or malt or lime, always with elaboration and set forms ; and many a London man has paid double and more for his violence and his greedy haste and very unchivalrous higgling. As happened with the land at Underwaltham, which the mortgagees had begged and implored the estate to take at twelve hundred, and had privately offered to all the world at a thousand, but which a sharp direct man, of the kind that makes great fortunes, a man in a motor-car, a man in a fur coat, a man of few words, bought for two thousand three hundred before my very eyes, protesting that they might take his offer or leave it ; and all because he did not begin by praising the land.

Well then, this man I spoke of offered to help me, and he went to get his scythe. But I went into the house and brought out a gallon jar of small ale for him and for me ; for the sun was now very warm, and small ale goes well with mowing. When we had drunk some of this ale in mugs called " I see you," we took each a swathe, he a little behind me because he was the better mower ; and so for many hours we swung, one before the other, mowing and mowing at the tall grass of the field. And the sun rose to noon and we were still at our mowing ; and we ate food, but only for a little while, and we took again to our mowing. And at last there was nothing left but a small square of grass, standing like a square of linesmen who keep their formation, tall and unbroken, with all the dead lying around them when the battle is over and done.

Then for some little time I rested after all

those hours; and the man and I talked together, and a long way off we heard in another field the musical sharpening of a scythe.

The sunlight slanted powdered and mellow over the breadth of the valley; for day was nearing its end. I went to fetch rakes from the steading; and when I had come back the last of the grass had fallen, and all the field lay flat and smooth, with the very green short grass in lanes between the dead and yellow swathes.

These swathes we raked into cocks to keep them from the dew against our return at daybreak; and we made the cocks as tall and steep as we could, for in that shape they best keep off the dew, and it is easier also to spread them after the sun has risen. Then we raked up every straggling blade, till the whole field was a clean floor for the tedding and the carrying of the hay next morning. The grass we had mown was but a little over two acres; for that is all the pasture on my little tiny farm.

When we had done all this, there fell upon us the beneficent and deliberate evening; so that as we sat a little while together near the rakes, we saw the valley more solemn and dim around us, and all the trees and hedgerows quite still, and held by a complete silence.

THE MOWING OF A FIELD

Then I paid my companion his wage, and bade him a good night, till we should meet in the same place before sunrise.

He went off with a slow and steady progress, as all our peasants do, making their walking a part of the easy but continual labour of their lives. But I sat on, watching the light creep around towards the north and change, and the waning moon coming up as though by stealth behind the woods of No Man's Land.

G. K. CHESTERTON
[1874–   ]

A PIECE OF CHALK *

I REMEMBER one splendid morning, all blue and silver, in the summer holidays, when I reluctantly tore myself away from the task of doing nothing in particular, and put on a hat of some sort and picked up a walking-stick, and put six very bright-coloured chalks in my pocket. I then went into the kitchen (which, along with the rest of the house, belonged to a very square and sensible old woman in a Sussex village), and asked the occupant and owner of the kitchen if she had any brown paper. She had a great deal ; in fact, she had too much ; and she mistook the purpose and the rationale of the existence of brown paper. She seemed to have an idea that if a person wanted brown paper he must be wanting to tie up parcels ; which was the last thing I wanted to do ; indeed, it is a thing which I have found to be beyond my mental

* From "Tremendous Trifles" (Methuen).

capacity. Hence she dwelt very much on the varying qualities of toughness and endurance in the material. I explained to her that I only wanted to draw pictures on it, and that I did not want them to endure in the least ; and that from my point of view, therefore, it was a question not of tough consistency, but of responsive surface, a thing comparatively irrelevant in a parcel. When she understood that I wanted to draw she offered to overwhelm me with notepaper, apparently supposing that I did my notes and correspondence on old brown paper wrappers from motives of economy.

I then tried to explain the rather delicate logical shade, that I not only liked brown paper, but liked the quality of brownness in paper, just as I liked the quality of brownness in October woods, or in beer, or in the peat-streams of the North. Brown paper represents the primal twilight of the first toil of creation, and with a bright-coloured chalk or two you can pick out points of fire in it, sparks of gold, and blood-red, and sea-green, like the first fierce stars that sprang out of divine darkness. All this I said (in an off-hand way) to the old woman ; and I put the brown paper in my pocket along with the chalks, and possibly other things. I suppose everyone must have reflected how primeval and how poetical are

the things that one carries in one's pocket ;
the pocket-knife, for instance, the type of all
human tools, the infant of the sword. Once
I planned to write a book of poems entirely
about the things in my pocket. But I found
it would be too long ; and the age of the great
epics is past.

*   *   *   *

With my stick and my knife, my chalks and
my brown paper, I went out on to the great
downs. I crawled across those colossal con-
tours that express the best quality of England,
because they are at the same time soft and
strong. The smoothness of them has the
same meaning as the smoothness of great cart-
horses, or the smoothness of the beech-tree ;
it declares in the teeth of our timid and cruel
theories that the mighty are merciful. As
my eye swept the landscape, the landscape
was as kindly as any of its cottages, but for
power it was like an earthquake. The villages
in the immense valley were safe, one could
see, for centuries ; yet the lifting of the whole
land was like the lifting of one enormous wave
to wash them all away.

I crossed one swell of living turf after
another, looking for a place to sit down and
draw. Do not, for heaven's sake, imagine I
was going to sketch from Nature. I was

going to draw devils and seraphim, and blind
old gods that men worshipped before the
dawn of right, and saints in robes of angry
crimson, and seas of strange green, and all the
sacred or monstrous symbols that look so well
in bright colours on brown paper. They are
much better worth drawing than Nature;
also they are much easier to draw. When a
cow came slouching by in the field next to
me, a mere artist might have drawn it; but
I always get wrong in the hind legs of
quadrupeds. So I drew the soul of the cow;
which I saw there plainly walking before me
in the sunlight; and the soul was all purple
and silver, and had seven horns and the
mystery that belongs to all the beasts. But
though I could not with a crayon get the best
out of the landscape, it does not follow that
the landscape was not getting the best out of
me. And this, I think, is the mistake that
people make about the old poets who lived
before Wordsworth, and were supposed not
to care very much about Nature because they
did not describe it much.

They preferred writing about great men to
writing about great hills; but they sat on the
great hills to write it. They gave out much
less about Nature, but they drank in, perhaps,
much more. They painted the white robes
of their holy virgins with the blinding snow,

at which they had stared all day. They blazoned the shields of their paladins with the purple and gold of many heraldic sunsets. The greenness of a thousand green leaves clustered into the live green figure of Robin Hood. The blueness of a score of forgotten skies became the blue robes of the Virgin. The inspiration went in like sunbeams and came out like Apollo.

*   *   *   *

But as I sat scrawling these silly figures on the brown paper, it began to dawn on me, to my great disgust, that I had left one chalk, and that a most exquisite and essential chalk, behind. I searched all my pockets, but I could not find any white chalk. Now, those who are acquainted with all the philosophy (nay, religion) which is typified in the art of drawing on brown paper, know that white is positive and essential. I cannot avoid remarking here upon a moral significance. One of the wise and awful truths which this brown-paper art reveals, is this, that white is a colour. It is not a mere absence of colour; it is a shining and affirmative thing, as fierce as red, as definite as black. When (so to speak) your pencil grows red-hot, it draws roses; when it grows white-hot, it draws stars. And one of the two or three defiant verities of the best religious morality, of real Christianity for example, is exactly this same thing ; the chief assertion of religious morality is that white is a colour. Virtue is not the absence of vices or the avoidance of moral dangers ; virtue is a vivid and separate thing, like pain or a particular smell. Mercy does not mean not being cruel or sparing people revenge or punishment ; it means a plain and positive thing like the sun, which one has either seen or not seen. Chastity does not mean abstention from sexual wrong ; it means something flaming, like Joan of Arc. In a word, God paints in many colours ; but He never paints so gorgeously, I had almost said so gaudily, as when He paints in white. In a sense our age has realised this fact, and expressed it in our sullen costume. For if it were really true that white was a blank and colourless thing, negative and non-committal, then white would be used instead of black and grey for the funeral dress of this pessimistic period. We should see city gentlemen in frock coats of spotless silver satin, with top hats as white as wonderful arum lilies. Which is not the case.

Meanwhile, I could not find my chalk.

* * * *

I sat on the hill in a sort of despair. There

was no town nearer than Chichester at which it was even remotely probable that there would be such a thing as an artist's colour-man. And yet, without white, my absurd little pictures would be as pointless as the world would be if there were no good people in it. I stared stupidly round, racking my brain for expedients. Then I suddenly stood up and roared with laughter, again and again, so that the cows stared at me and called a committee. Imagine a man in the Sahara regretting that he had no sand for his hour-glass. Imagine a gentleman in mid-ocean wishing that he had brought some salt water with him for his chemical experiments. I was sitting on an immense warehouse of white chalk. The landscape was made entirely out of white chalk. White chalk was piled mere miles until it met the sky. I stooped and broke a piece off the rock I sat on : it did not mark so well as the shop chalks do ; but it gave the effect. And I stood there in a trance of pleasure, realising that this Southern England is not only a grand peninsula, and a tradition and a civilisation ; it is something even more admirable. It is a piece of chalk.

ROBERT LYND

[1879–   ]

THE SHY FATHERS *

IT is difficult to refuse a child's invitation, even when it is to attend the breaking-up ceremony at a school. At first, I pleaded shyness; but my niece said with a pout, "That's what all the men say. Elizabeth says her father's shy, but she's simply going to make him come; and Ann's father says *he's* too shy, but Ann's going to make him come, too. Why should all the fathers be shy?" "I don't know anything about the fathers," I told her; "I can only answer for the uncles." "Well, why should uncles be shy?" That, I confess, bowled me. "Oh, well," I said, "I'll come along with the shy fathers."

I admit I should not have gone if I had not been fairly sure that the shy fathers would be there in considerable numbers. The thought of being present in a large schoolroom, with no

* From "The Blue Lion" (Methuen).

other man present, in the midst of a throng
of far from shy women and children, I find
terrifying to the imagination. It is not that
I dislike the company of women and children ;
on the whole, I think it is the best company
in the world. But, as Bacon has said, a
crowd is not company, and the loneliness of a
man entirely surrounded by women and
children surpasses even the loneliness of a
man isolated in the middle of the Sahara.
Apart from this, however, I think there are
several reasons for the shyness of fathers
when they are pressed by their children to
go to a breaking-up party. The average
father, I suspect, is afraid of what his children's
school friends may think of him. He knows
that, by the grace of God, his own children
do not see him as he really is. They play
games with him as with an equal. They laugh
at least at some of his jokes. They appear at
times to regard him as the richest, the bravest
and the cleverest man in the world. Has
not one boasted of one's own father ? I
remember at the age of eight boasting to a
bosom friend that my father was a multi-
millionaire. He had boastfully said that his
father had a million pounds. I said that my
father had three. And, for all I knew, it
might have been true. A child, indeed, is
reluctant to believe that there may be fathers

in the world superior in any way to its own.
A friend of mine, an occasional writer of
mediocre verse, was referring to some story
about Blake the other day, when his ten-year-
old daughter interrupted him to ask who
Blake was. "Oh, he was a genius—wrote
'Tiger, tiger,'" said her father. "Was he
as big a genius as you?" inquired the little
girl. "Good gracious, you mustn't call me
a genius!" he told her. "*I* think you are,"
she said, gently but firmly. "Why"—he
explained the situation—"I couldn't write
'Tiger, tiger,' if I lived to be a thousand."
"I would rather have 'O Bonar, Bonar, why
thus dishonour?'" she told him, quoting the
first line of a set of atrocious political verses
he had written. Of such is the kingdom of
Heaven.

I do not, I may say, suggest that a father
never sees the little waves of criticism stealing
into his child's face, or that he has any reason
to fear that his child is likely, for any long
period of time, to mistake him for a god. He
knows that the process of finding him out
may be a slow one, but that it is cumulative
and that it is sure. But he also knows that
his child, as a rule, over-estimates him in a
way in which no other child would. That is
why, when he is asked to submit himself to
the critical eyes of his children's schoolfellows,

he feels suddenly shy and apprehensive. No man may be able to add a cubit to his stature, but he has an uneasy suspicion that the eyes of other people's children may be able to take several cubits off. Even so, I do not think that it is mainly an injury to his vanity that the shy father fears. After all, if other people's children do not like him, he can always avenge himself by disliking them twice as much. It is chiefly on his children's account that he feels shy. Being sentimental, he feels —or pretends to feel—that he is unworthy to be the father of such wonderful children, and he shrinks from saddling them with a second-rate parent in presence of their friends. He must look, he tells himself, an odd sort of fish, and though, heaven knows, all the other fathers of his acquaintance look as odd sorts of fish as you could wish to meet, still he does not like the notion of an odd sort of fish being seen in public as the father of these particular children. He would hate to see his children appearing in ridiculous clothes ; he hates equally the thought of their appearing with a ridiculous parent.

There is, I am told, no greater happiness known on earth than that of a father who, after a party to which his children's school friends have been invited, can lie back in his chair and tell himself that he did not behave so badly after all. It is always pleasant to pass an examination, but there is no examination which it is a more blessed relief to pass than an examination by one's children's friends. Fathers have told me of the nervousness they have seen in their children on such occasions—of the impatient expression they have observed on the little face that, at a joke that has no point or that has a point that nobody is able to see, tells them of the silent soliloquy : " Daddy being silly again ! " Pity the tremors of children for their fathers. Pity the tremors of fathers for themselves. Happy is the child whose father acquits himself with credit in the presence of its friends. How delightful it was in one's childhood to see one's own father being a success in such trying circumstances ! One cheered in one's soul as he, habitually a silent man, awoke out of his silence into the most fascinating conversationalist, made jokes that were good jokes, and told stories of his experiences that were better than a book. There was no personal triumph to surpass the triumph of having such a father as this. To see the faces of one's friends brightening made, I am sure, one's own face bright. Some children, on the other hand, even children who are devoted to their fathers, accustom themselves from an early age to the knowledge that their fathers are imperfect creatures whose faults must be put up with as the decree of destiny. I knew one boy whose father, an excellent and interesting man, had the fault of talking too much and of telling a story at twice the length at which it ought to have been told. The boy never showed the slightest irritation, as many boys would have done. When the father had lost his bearings in the middle of an apparently endless anecdote the boy would merely say, with a smile, " Ring off, governor !" and turn the conversation to another subject. It is not in every home, however, that the long-winded elderly and the impatient young are on such good terms as to be able to face such a situation, not only once, but again and again, without getting to dislike each other. I should myself have been tempted to play the Roman father in such circumstances. For a man may forgive many wrongs, but he cannot easily forgive anyone who makes it plain that his conversation is tedious. " We can forgive those who bore us," said La Rochefoucauld ; " we cannot forgive those whom we bore." It was, I suppose, my sense of the enormity of the implied accusation that made me, even in the midst of an unusually long anecdote, always sympathise with the long-winded father, even more warmly than I agreed with the " Ring off, governor ! " of the boy.

THE SHY FATHERS

I cannot say that I set out for the school with any intention of making my niece proud of me, but I was buoyed up by the hope that I should not actually disgrace her. As a matter of fact, I do not think there was any chance of disgracing her, unless one had risen from one's chair and made a scene. The shy man usually finds that he has been shy without a cause, and that, in practice, no one takes the slightest notice of him. Sitting in the back row against the wall, indeed, I could watch the children, all costumed as for the stage, going through their dances, their songs, and their plays in almost complete self-forgetfulness, without even troubling to look round to see how the shy fathers were getting on.

To see a play performed by small children with a few footlights arranged on the floor in imitation of a theatre, is to feel that all that the saints have said about children is true. How exquisite are their voices, that are all music without the harshness of experience! To listen to them is like listening to the first birds. To see them is to be back in a world of apple trees in flower. There is comedy in the contrast between them, and the grave parts they play and the grave speeches they utter as abbesses, poets, and harpers. But the very mimicry of our grown-up world, which begins by moving us, ends by filling us with

ROBERT LYND

bitter-sweet regret that the lives of men and
women, after all, are not enacted in voices so
sweet and by creatures so fair as these. The
feeling may not be a deep one, and may be
only for the moment ; but, for the time at
least, we wish with a pang that life could
always have remained like this, that nobody
would ever grow up or die, but that the very
kings and admirals and prime ministers and
thieves and shopkeepers were all children. It
may be that, from the point of view of those
who have passed into further æons of existence,
kings and admirals and prime ministers and
thieves and shopkeepers are so. Who knows
but that, in immortal eyes, a conqueror
marching from ruined kingdom to ruined kingdom may be but a small boy with a toy sword
at his side ? After all, the grey-haired and
the bald play their parts in almost as complete
innocence of what they are doing as these
children, who at least know that it is all a
game. And, indeed, the contrast between a
child of twelve and a grown-up human being
is scarcely greater than the contrast between
a child of five or six and a child of twelve.
I had never realised the enormous gap between
six and twelve till a band of little six-year-old
dancers came on to the stage with solemn feet
and solemn faces and went through their steps
in the middle of a half-circle of girls, none of

THE SHY FATHERS

whom was older than twelve and none younger than ten. Kings, Puritans, Cavaliers, mackerel-sellers, and cut-purses of twelve seemed six feet high in comparison with these midget elves. They, too, seemed infinitely small and of a perfect age when they were on the stage alone, but the children of six had only to appear in order to let me see that there was an age still nearer perfection. Not that I should care to be dogmatic on this point. It may be only a passing ripple of sentimentalism that makes one wish that all the world were of so doll-like a stature as this, and that the very editor of "The Times" were a little fellow of six. There are others, perhaps, who would regard the little elf of six as a giant compared to the sleeping infant in long clothes—the infant in the comet stage, as Meredith saw it. The child in the cradle is, for many people, the eternal Sleeping Beauty, and, if one may judge by religious art, it is the age that to men of imagination has seemed most divine. I confess I am content with six—nay, with seven, or eight, or nine, or ten, or eleven, or twelve. And, perhaps, there may be something to be said for any age up to sixteen, or even twenty, or, at a stretch, thirty, and if you advance the age to forty I shall not quarrel with you. There is, within these limits, no year that would not be better if it lasted at least three

307

years ; but I am not sure that, at the age of six, a year should not last ten. It may be that if all these children, six and twelve alike, had not been doomed to grow old, I should not have been so moved at the spectacle of their grace and the sweet sound of their voices. And if I myself had remained at their age I might only have squabbled with them and seen some of them not as angels but with a hostile eye. Hence all may be for the best in the best of all possible worlds, and it may be that to be an uncle appears as wonderful a destiny to a little girl of ten as to be a little girl of ten seems to an uncle. In any case I shall tell my niece that I think the perfect age is not six, but ten. An uncle has only one duty—to make himself popular with his nephews and nieces.

NOTES

STEELE [1672–1729].—Sir Richard Steele, essayist and dramatist, fitly heads any list of English essay-writers because it was he who founded *The Tatler* in 1709 and made this kind of writing popular, and it was he, more than any other man, who made the essay his confessional. He strikes the most intimate note to be found in the English essay before Lamb. Steele was something of a scatter-brain, for ever sinning and repenting, but the very qualities that stood in his way in any other kind of writing were perhaps in his favour as an essayist. His natural impulsiveness broke through the stilted manner of his time, and though the majority of his *Tatler* and *Spectator* papers are not so good as Addison's, simply because their author was not such an accomplished man of letters as his friend, the best of them are superior to Addison's best. They have a tenderness and charm and knowledge of human character unsurpassed in the essay for a hundred years following the first appearance of *The Tatler*. There is too in the style a certain playfulness, the result of writing from the heart and making the reader an old friend, that gives the prose an appeal not to be found elsewhere during that age. "The great charm of Steele's writing is its naturalness," Thackeray remarks. "He wrote so quickly and carelessly that he was forced to make the reader his confidant and had not the time to

deceive him." The essays included in this volume
are Nos. 95 and 181 of *The Tatler* and No. 2 of *The
Spectator* respectively. It will be noticed that
though it was Addison who developed the idea of
Sir Roger and his associates, it was Steele who began
it. There are a good many selections of his essays
in existence.

ADDISON [1672–1719].—Addison was a far greater figure
than his friend Steele, and, as statesman, poet,
dramatist, critic, and essayist, was one of the most
admired and successful English men of letters of
the eighteenth century. His essays are chiefly
remarkable for their charming, easy, polished manner
and style, and their all-pervading good humour.
Although Steele introduced him to periodical writing,
it was Addison who did most of the work, particularly
on *The Spectator*, which is almost entirely his. The
essays here are all from *The Spectator*, being Nos. 112,
335 and 517, and they form an interesting link
between fiction, which at the time these papers were
written, could show nothing so intimate, nothing at
once so humorous and pathetic, and the essay proper.
His style was regarded as a perfect model of English
prose during the hundred years following its appearance, and among its foremost admirers was Dr.
Johnson, who said : " Whoever wishes to attain an
English style, familiar, but not coarse, and elegant
but not ostentatious, must give his days and nights
to the volumes of Addison." Since this was written,
there has been a considerable fall in Addison's stock,
but it would still be difficult to overpraise these Sir
Roger papers.

SWIFT [1667–1745].—I have put Swift after Steele and
Addison because, though he was senior to them,
their position as essayists entitles them to the first
place. Swift was a greater man than either, but
that terrible indignation of his turned him away

NOTES

from the familiar essay to the pamphlet and the satirical narrative. But he contributed an occasional *Tatler* and *Spectator* paper, and the essay here is from No. 20 of *The Tatler*. It is not included in my edition (Bohn's) of *The Tatler*, and I found it in the complete edition of Swift's works edited by Hawksworth. This amusing paper is far more like those of his colleagues than are the others by Swift, but it hits harder and, as most readers who have accepted many kinds of hospitality will readily agree, it will be some time yet before it lacks a target for its satire.

JOHNSON [1709–1784].—Johnson to us is a great figure, a colossal character, rather than a great literary man. It is the man who talks in Boswell's Life who interests us and not the man who wrote innumerable *Ramblers* and *Idlers* and *Adventurers*. Actually Johnson's periodical work is far more readable than is generally imagined, but it must be confessed that it is too impersonal and pompous to be really enjoyable. Of the two sets of papers written by Johnson, *The Rambler* and *The Idler*, the latter is much lighter in tone and more entertaining. The essay selected here, however, is from neither, but forms No. 84 of *The Adventurer*, and will be unfamiliar to most readers. Though it begins badly, in the old pompous fashion, it becomes lighter and more personal towards the close. Actually Johnson ought to have written his best on this subject because, as all readers of Boswell know, riding in a coach was one of his favourite pleasures. There is not a better example, however, of that impersonal tendency (mentioned in the Introduction) which bleached so much of the work of the eighteenth century periodical writers, than this periodical work of Johnson's, because he was a born essayist. If he had only written as he talked, he would have been a great essayist.

311

NOTES

GOLDSMITH [1728–1774].—Goldsmith must be accounted one of the most felicitous men of letters in English Literature, for everything he wrote, no matter whether fiction, drama, verse or essays, he wrote exquisitely, apparently without effort. These two sketches of Beau Tibbs are taken from his *Citizen of the World*, a series of letters purported to be written by a Chinese visitor to this country. The scheme was a familiar one, but Goldsmith, as usual, achieved a kind of perfection. In the same way, the little hanger-on of fashion, the beggarly dandy, is a familiar figure in eighteenth century literature, but Beau Tibbs transcends the mere type and stands by himself. It is the odd fleeting pathos that makes these sketches tower above other things of this kind of the period.

LAMB [1775–1834].—Probably the most widely-loved figure in our literature. His *Essays of Elia*, from which these three papers are taken, are the very essence of this kind of writing; they are drenched in the unusual personality of their writer; even the smallest turn of phrase is individual. The three essays selected here show his extraordinary range, from the lightest and oddest generalisations to the most intimate personal revelations only covered by the thinnest veil of fiction. But Lamb cannot be selected, for there are few things that anyone who knows the essays would be ready to set aside and probably no two readers would agree as to what those few were. It is worth noticing how immensely the essay gains by the change in prose form from a somewhat impersonal classical manner to the looser, richer, more romantic and personal manner. Style in Lamb, while it has all the little felicities of phrase of the best of the earlier styles, has become a voice, and to be properly appreciated it must sound in your ear as you read. Once that happens,

312

it is almost magical, and his humour and whimsical
pathos are immensely heightened. Lamb was very
often called " the inimitable " in his own day, and
for once this term is no hyperbole, for he is strictly
inimitable. But his influence on subsequent essayists
has been enormous. Indeed, he may be said to
have set the fashion in essay-writing. Thus, to
take only one example, the device of making the
most of one's weaknesses, of exaggerating one's
ignorance or laziness and so forth, a device very
common in modern essays, probably owes its existence
to Lamb, who was certainly the first essayist to
make extended use of it. That is why the reader
should correct his impression of *Elia* by a study
of Lamb's life, for it was the more irresponsible
and whimsical side of his character that he exploited
in his essays, which were to him a kind of moral
and intellectual holiday. There was in Lamb a
curious mixture of opposites, for he was at once
a Bohemian and yet a kind of exquisite Quaker-like
puritan, a man who seemed to follow any and every
whim and yet a man with a most rigid sense of honour,
and so on and so forth. He is so individual that he
presents us with a unity, yet within this unity there
is unusual variety. This is one, and not the least,
secret of his charm and unfailing appeal. All readers
of the *Essays* should go forward to the *Letters,* which
some critics consider even better than the essays,
of which they are a kind of extension.

HAZLITT [1778–1830].—Hazlitt's place is with Lamb, at the
very head of the essayists. His note is gusto, an
amazing power of loving and hating, praising and
blaming, an extraordinary capacity for being disgusted or falling into an ecstasy. There is no other
writer attacks a subject with quite the same abandon,
and yet there are few writers more capable of keeping
their heads on their shoulders. All his essays are,

as it were, a kind of red-hot meditation. And as a purely descriptive writer, he has probably no equal. For years, so he tells us, he found it impossible to express himself adequately in words. He could think, but he could not write. He was past thirty before he had begun to find his feet. But having once found them, we may say that he never stopped running. His words seem ever on the point of bolting, yet he always manages to keep a hand on the reins. We know how he used to rise about noon, brew great quantities of very strong tea and then sit before his fire, sipping his tea and meditating through the afternoon. He would then set to work and write steadily for hours, never stopping, never hesitating, never altering a word, each sheet ready for the printer as soon as his pen had reached the bottom. Other persons have had this gusto, but Hazlitt has the power of communicating it to his reader, so that we read his work in much the same fashion as he wrote it, headlong, eager, and yet always alert, never quite unbalanced. His chief faults are repetition, of both ideas and phrases, and a certain rattling monotony in his style when he is below his usual level. Hazlitt has suffered, perhaps more than most essayists, from hackneyed selection of his work, for such things as " Going a Journey " and " The Indian Jugglers " have been chosen too often. Of the two essays included in this volume, the first, " Merry England," comes from *Essays and Sketches,* and the second, " The Fight," an essay that is always singled out for praise by critics of Hazlitt but that is rarely seen, first appeared in the *New Monthly Magazine* in 1822, and only appeared in book form, in his *Literary Remains,* after Hazlitt's death. It is an astonishing piece of bravura writing and undoubtedly the best specimen of its kind in existence. There are any number of

NOTES

editions of Hazlitt's various volumes of essays to be had, and also two volumes of selections, one, a very full one, edited by Alexander Ireland and now only to be found in second-hand book shops, and the other a recent production edited by Mr. P. P. Howe, the author of a very fine life of Hazlitt.

LEIGH HUNT [1784-1859].—Flimsier than either Lamb's or Hazlitt's, Leigh Hunt's essays are practically all short and hasty performances, obviously written at the last moment. They have not the range, the depth, the personality of the other men's essays, and Hunt never goes down into himself for hidden treasure, so to speak, as Lamb and Hazlitt do. He glides, very gracefully, over the surface of life and art. But he has humour and a pleasant fancy, and here and there a genuine touch of pathos (though often inclining to the mawkish), and he sketches his world as it passes more surely than either of his greater contemporaries. These two little papers of his are taken from *The Indicator,* a very belated blossom of the *Tatler* tree. Hunt gains immensely by a judicious selection, preferably on the small side, of his essays, and fortunately there are several in existence.

THACKERAY [1811-1863].—Thackeray, as I have remarked in the Introduction, is a born essayist. Even his novels, with the exception of *Barry Lyndon* and *Esmond* and *The Virginians,* are a kind of extended essay, for what is most apparent in them is the personality of the writer, which is not only not concealed, as it is in most novels, but is actually emphasised. Everything that Thackeray wrote, whether it was a story or a book review or a skit for *Punch,* is saturated in his individuality. The secret of Thackeray's charm lies in his style, a true essayist's style, a real personal voice. It is a style that appears to run on easily and almost lazily,

NOTES

quite unpretentious and demanding no special attention on the part of the reader, and yet he can do almost anything with it, from the gravest irony, the most mournful abandon, to the lightest laughter. It is a style devised not for the eye but for the ear, its appeal being one of rhythm and cadence. It will probably be found, on examination, that the persons for whom Thackeray has no charm as a writer, and there are a great number of them now, are without an ear for prose. Although he was by nature an essayist, Thackeray did not, however, write a great many actual essays. When he was appointed editor of *The Cornhill* magazine, he contributed a series of *Roundabout Papers* to its pages, and these form his only set of essays proper. It is from this series that the essay here has been chosen.

ALEXANDER SMITH [1830–1867].—Smith began as a poet, and was for a time foolishly overpraised and considered a possible rival to Tennyson. The result of this was a quick reaction, from which his poetry, which lacks force and real imaginative power but is by no means without merit, has never recovered. Towards the end of his short life, he turned to prose, producing some fiction and one volume of essays, *Dreamthorpe*, from which " A Lark's Flight " has been taken. Smith's essays are better than his poetry, and had he lived he might possibly have become one of the major essayists of the century, but his work, as it stands, lacks body and personality. Even so, however, it deserves a larger public than it has had, particularly as it has a broad rather than profound appeal, both in its matter and manner.

R. L. STEVENSON [1850–1894].—It is still an open question whether Stevenson was really an essayist trying to write fiction or a novelist pretending to write essays. Nearly all critics have made up their minds that he was one or the other, and will not allow him the double capacity. On the whole, the present writer sides with those who (like Mr. Saintsbury, who knew Stevenson when he was hesitating between the two forms and told him to choose the novel) see in him a writer of fiction first and an essayist afterwards. It is as well to remember, though, that he gave to fiction his matured powers, and that a large number of his essays only represent his 'prentice work. It is more than likely that, had he lived, he would have returned to the essay and made it his own. For some curious reason, he is always represented, as an essayist, by the earlier and flimsier work, the "Walking Tours" and the rest, whereas his best work in this form, the series he contributed to *Scribners'* during the eighties, is nearly always neglected. The gem of this series, in my opinion, is the essay included here—"The Lantern Bearers"—which not only captures, with his usual felicity, a boyish experience, but enables him to express his romantic view of life more fully and, I think, more soundly than he ever expressed it elsewhere. The style, too, in these later things is better than it is in the earlier essays, for it has all the lilt and glitter and curious eager delicacy, without the appearance of being over-mannered, the suggestion of the velvet jacket.

E. V. LUCAS [1868-   ].—Mr. Lucas is one of our most prolific essayists, with an unusually wide range of interests and an urbane and unruffled manner that conceals a certain sardonic humour that, unfortunately, I think, has never been given full expression. His appearance of almost flippant ease conceals too, particularly in the earlier volumes, a good deal of very fine craftsmanship. One sometimes regrets that Mr. Lucas has, as it were, spread the substance of his work out so thinly and evenly and denied it a stiffening of ideas, of intellectual body, that would have raised it high above even the best journalism,

NOTES

but even such regrets are somewhat ungrateful for Mr. Lucas has given more pleasure to a large body of cultivated readers than almost any other miscellaneous writer of our time, and is a perfect companion for an idle hour. He has made at least one selection from his own work (*A Little of Everything*), but even now he would probably gain by a judicious selection, for here and there are outstanding essays that disarm all criticism. Among them, the little essay, in dramatic form, included here must take a high place, for of its kind it is perfect. Mr. Lucas is an authority on Charles Lamb, and his life of the essayist is one of the very best biographies this age has produced.

HILAIRE BELLOC [1870-   ].—There is certainly no lack of either body or personality in the essays of Mr. Belloc, which are unusually varied, ranging from grave little historical treatises to wild scraps of satire, so varied indeed that it is nothing short of unjust to try and represent him by one essay, and yet although they are so varied are obviously the work of one man, so steeped are they in the strong individuality of their creator. What chiefly distinguishes them is a certain massive concreteness in the style, which has a curiously timeless air, for though it does not read like something written to-day, neither is it definitely archaic. At its best, his prose is very fine indeed ; one of the best prose styles of our time, but his manner is apt to become a little wearisome if he is not writing his best because it lacks light and shade. He, too, is more often than not discovered hiding himself, behind a fictitious " I " he has invented, rather than revealing himself, and is too often tempted to become a hectoring schoolmaster (though, of course, a good deal of his bullying and arrogance is " only his fun ") rather than a friend. His best work is to be found in *Hills and the*

NOTES

Sea (from which the essay here is taken, and which mainly consists of travel essays), and *On Something* and *On Nothing*.

G. K. CHESTERTON [1874–   ].—Mr. Chesterton's most remarkable characteristics, as an essayist, are his all-pervading humour, his genuine romantic and poetical sense of wonder, which enables him to see things freshly, from a new angle, as he does in the essay in this selection, and his wealth of ideas. His greatest fault is his trick, noted in the Introduction, of pretending to embark upon a confession, a genuine piece of autobiography, and really leading the reader into a debate, or rather having him ambushed by a set of opinions. His style, too, is not sufficiently exact and concrete, has not, as it were, sufficient integrity, to be that of a great essayist. He will always have a place among essayists, but he will have a more important one among the great controversialists. His earlier volumes are better, from our point of view, than the later, and the best of them are *The Defendant, Tremendous Trifles* (from which the essay here has been taken) and *All Things Considered*. Many of the topics dealt with in these volumes were things of the moment, whose interest has long since passed, but the laughter and the wonder and the amazing play of ideas that Mr. Chesterton lavished upon them keep these papers from decay, for laughter and wonder and genuine ideas do not stale.

ROBERT LYND [1879–   ].—Mr. Lynd is essentially a writer of to-day, that is, he writes of the things we know, of buses, race-meetings, cricket-matches, seaside hotels, patent medicines, and anything that happens to interest him in the life stirring about him ; and he writes like a man of this age, from the angle of the early twentieth century. Yet he is incontestably in the tradition of the great English essayists. He does not write like Hazlitt or Lamb,

NOTES

but he is doing for us what Hazlitt or Lamb did for his age, and the tradition lives in him. He paints his own portrait for us. And in doing this, he does more, for he takes all the little topics of the moment, the little crazes, the shows and spectacles, describes them, moralises—ever so lightly and surely—over them, and so links them up to the great background of life. There is no modern essayist who is better able to connect particular things with general ideas, who is better able to play at one and the same time the spectator, the humorist and the moralist. We can end this volume with him because the great tradition, of which he is the latest heir of any importance, is safe with him : the English Essay, whose fortunes we have followed, is still in existence, still coming into existence, and readers of those little volumes bearing Mr. Lynd's name, *The Pleasures of Ignorance*, *Solomon in All His Glory*, *The Blue Lion*, and *The Peal of Bells*, are well aware of the fact.

J. B. P.